welcome

With a project for every knitter (from novice to experienced), you're bound to find inspiration here in this exciting collection. Start small and easy with a striped hat or a scarf. Work up to an afghan or ribbed cardigan. And for those who want a challenge, give advanced projects a try—a Fair Isle and cable hat, scarf, and gloves will be the exquisite rewards of your hard work.

In this guide to knitting, you'll find all the help you'll need. Look for specific stitch instructions, abbreviations, and a list of general supplies on pages 46 and 47. Diagrams and finished photos will keep you on track, too, and each design is clearly labeled by skill level to help you choose projects that are right for you. To further assist you, yarn and color suggestions accompany each project—but don't be afraid to substitute other yarns and colors. As long as you use a yarn in the same weight category and you work to gauge, you'll be successful.

We encourage you to have fun and try something new. Whether you're adding embroidery to a garment, knitting furry yarn into a sweater, or felting a pair of slippers and a flowered tote, you'll come away with the pride of a project well done.

happy knitting!

Page 28

Page 32

Page 42

contents

homespun comfort

Watch subtle bands of color arise as this vertical stripe pattern with a garter-stitch border grows.

DESIGNER: LION BRAND YARN COMPANY PHOTOGRAPHERS: SCOTT LITTLE, *BELOW;* ANDY LYONS, *OPPOSITE*

SKILL LEVEL
Beginner

FINISHED MEASUREMENTS
Approx 45×50"

YARNS
Lion Brand Homespun (Art. 790);
98% acrylic/2% polyester; 6 oz. (170 g);
185 yds. (167 m); bulky weight
- 3 skeins #322 Baroque
- 3 skeins #319 Adirondack

NEEDLES
- Size 15 (12 mm) 29" circular needle, *or size needed to obtain gauge*

GAUGE
Holding 1 strand of each yarn tog, in pattern, 10 sts and 24 rows = 6" (15 cm). TAKE TIME TO CHECK YOUR GAUGE.

Note: The entire afghan is worked back and forth on a circular needle with a double strand of yarn.

INSTRUCTIONS
With 1 strand of each yarn held tog, cast on 75 sts. K 7 rows for Garter st border.
Row 1 (RS): Knit.
Row 2: K4; (p2, k3) 13 times, p2, k4.
Rep Rows 1 and 2 until throw measures approx 49" from beg, ending with a RS row. K 7 rows for Garter st border. Bind off.

V-neck classics

Up-front styling makes these cardigans as great-looking as they are practical to wear.

Shawl-Collar Chic

DESIGNER: MARY MARIK
PHOTOGRAPHER: PERRY STRUSE

SKILL LEVEL

Intermediate

SIZES

S (M, L, XL, 2X, 3X)
Shown in Size L. The pattern is written for the smallest size with changes for larger sizes in parentheses. When only one number is given, it applies to all sizes.
Note: For ease in working, circle all numbers pertaining to the size you're making.

FINISHED MEASUREMENTS

Underarm = 40 (44, 48, 52, 56, 60)"

YARNS

Lion Brand Jiffy (Art. 450); 100% acrylic; 3 oz. (85 g); 135 yds. (123 m); bulky weight

- 5 (5, 6, 7, 7, 8) balls #151 Oxford Gray (A)
- 3 (3, 4, 4, 5, 6) balls #153 Black (B)

NEEDLES & EXTRAS

- Size 10 (6 mm) needles
- Size 10.5 (6.5 mm) needles *or size needed to obtain gauge*
- Size 10 (6 mm) 29" circular needle
- Stitch markers
- Stitch holders
- Blunt-end yarn needle
- Five 1⅜"-long buttons

GAUGE

12 sts and 17 rows = 4" (10 cm) over St st (knit 1 row, purl 1 row), using larger needles. TAKE TIME TO CHECK YOUR GAUGE.
Note: Work all incs 1 st in from edge.

INSTRUCTIONS

BACK

With larger needles and B, cast on 60 (66, 72, 78, 84, 90) sts. Change to smaller needles and work in Garter st (k every row) for 6", ending with a WS row.
Change to larger needles and A, and cast on 1 st at beg and end of row—62 (68, 74, 80, 86, 92) sts.
Note: Extra edge stitches are selvedges. Work even in St st until piece measures 18 (19, 19½, 19½, 20, 20)" from beg.
Shape armholes: At beg of the next 2 rows, bind off 4 (4, 6, 6, 8, 8) sts—54 (60, 62, 68, 70, 76) sts. Work even until armholes measure 7 (7, 8, 8, 9, 10)", ending with a WS row.
Shape back of neck: K22 (25, 25, 28, 28, 31) sts, join in 2nd ball of yarn, bind off 10 (10, 12, 12, 14, 14) center sts, k22 (25, 25, 28, 28, 31) sts. Working both sides at the same time, bind off 6 (7, 6, 7, 7, 7) sts at each neck edge once, 6 (6, 6, 7, 6, 7) sts once, then 4 (6, 6, 6, 6, 7) sts. Work even until piece measures 9 (9, 10, 10, 11, 12)" from beg of armhole. Place rem 6 (6, 7, 8, 9, 10) shoulder sts on holders.

LEFT FRONT

With larger needles and B, cast on 22 (25, 28, 30, 33, 36) sts. Change to smaller needles and work in Garter st for 6". Change to larger needles and A, and cast on 1 st at side edge (for selvedge)—23 (26, 29, 31, 34, 37) sts. Work even in St st until piece measures 18 (19, 19½, 19½, 20, 20)" from beg, ending with a WS row.
Shape armhole: Bind off 4 (4, 6, 6, 8, 8) sts at beg of next row—19 (22, 23, 25, 26, 29) sts. P back.
Begin front neckline shaping—Dec Row: K to last 3 sts, k2tog, k1. Work Dec Row every other row 12 (15, 15, 16, 16, 18) times more—6 (6, 7, 8, 9, 10) sts. When piece measures same as Back, put shoulder sts on holder.

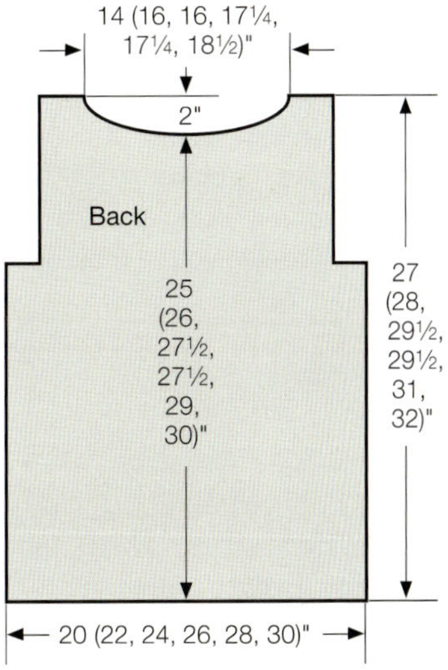

RIGHT FRONT

Work same as Left Front, reversing shaping.
Begin front neckline shaping—Dec Row: K1, ssk, knit to end of row.

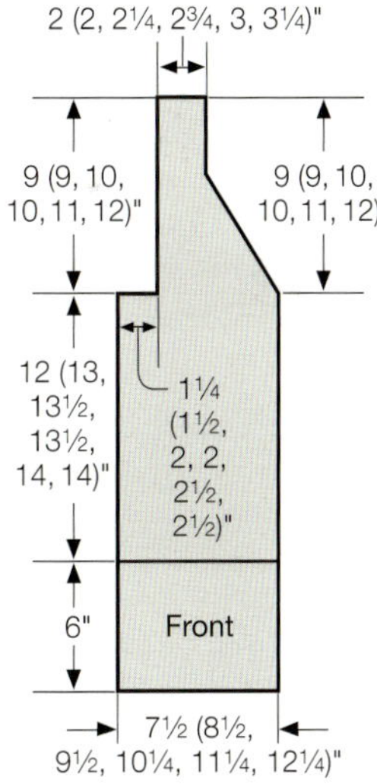

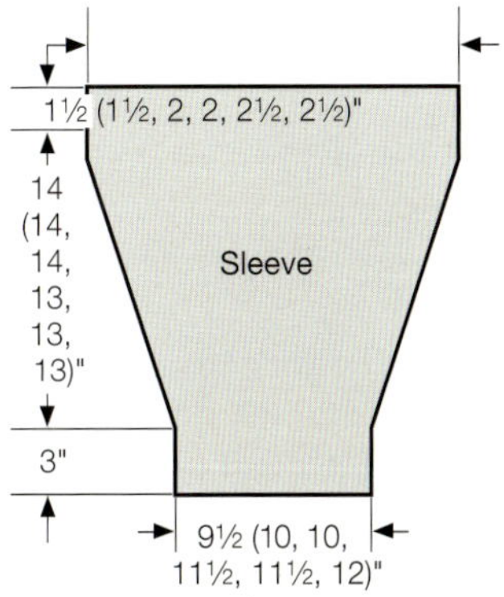

SLEEVE (make 2)

With larger needles and B, cast on 28 (30, 30, 34, 34, 36) sts. Change to smaller needles and work in Garter st for 3", ending with a WS row. Change to larger needles and A, and beg St st, inc 1 st at each end of first row and then every 4th row 13 (12, 14, 12, 9, 7) times, then every 2nd row 0 (0, 0, 0, 6, 10) times—56 (56, 60, 60, 66, 72) sts. Work even until piece measures 17 (17, 17, 16, 16, 16)" or desired length to underarm. Work even for an additional 1½ (1½, 2, 2, 2½, 2½)". Bind off loosely.

FINISHING

With RS tog, join shoulders with three-needle bind-off, *page 47*. Sew in Sleeves. Sew sleeve seams and side seams to top of bottom band, leaving a 6" opening. Mark positions for 5 buttonholes evenly spaced along Right Front between 6" bottom band and front neck shaping.

Front Band: With RS facing, smaller circular needle and B, beg at lower edge of Right Front and pick up and k53 (56, 58, 58, 60, 60) sts along straight edge, 23 (24, 25, 25, 27, 30) sts along shaped neck edge, 42 (48, 48, 52, 52, 56) sts along back neck edge, 23 (24, 25, 25, 27, 30) sts along shaped neck edge, and 53 (56, 58, 58, 60, 60) sts along straight edge—194 (208, 214, 218, 226, 236) sts.

Next row (WS): K to within 3 sts of shoulder seam, pm, k16 (18, 18, 19, 19, 20) sts, place marker (pm), k16 (18, 18, 20, 20, 22) sts, k to 3 sts after shoulder seam, pm, k to end. Back neck of jacket is now divided into 3 roughly equal sections.

Shape back of neckline band: Cont in Garter st.

Rows 3, 5, and 7 (RS): Work 1 dec (k2tog) in each back neck section. *Note: Distribute these decs and those on following rows in a random manner.*

Row 9: Work 2 decs in each back neck section.

Rows 11, 13, and 15: Work 1 dec in each back neck section.

Row 17: Work 2 decs in each back neck section.

Rows 19 and 21: Work 1 dec in each back neck section. AT SAME TIME, on Row 21, make yo, k2tog buttonholes at positions marked for buttons. Approx 161 (175, 181, 185, 193, 203) sts remain on needle.

Row 23: Inc 1 st in each back neckline section.

Row 24: K across, removing stitch markers.

Shawl Collar—Row 25: K until you reach beg of front shaping on Left Front.

Wrap next stitch as follows: Sl next st pwise to right needle, bring yarn from back to front, then pass st back to left needle unworked. Turn.

Row 26: K to beg of front shaping on Right Front. Wrap stitch; turn.

Row 27: K to within 4 sts of wrapped st on Left Front, wrap next st, and turn.

Row 28: Work to within 4 sts of wrapped st on Right Front, wrap, and turn. Cont in this manner, always knitting to within 4 sts of previously wrapped st for approx 5 wrap-and-turns on each front edge, ending with a final wrap-and-turn a few sts below the shoulder seam on the Right Front. *Note: There should be an equal number of wrap-and-turns on each front.*

Next row (RS): K all the way to lower edge of Left Front, knitting wrapped sts in normal fashion. Change to large needle and bind off front band and shawl collar loosely. *Note: If you have a needle 2 sizes larger, use this to bind off, especially across back of neck.* Weave in ends. Sew on buttons.

Easy-Going Rib

DESIGNER: KATHY ZIMMERMAN
PHOTOGRAPHER: PERRY STRUSE

SKILL LEVEL

beginner+

SIZES

XS (S, M, L, XL, 2X)

Shown in Size M. The pattern is written for the smallest size with changes for larger sizes in parentheses. When only one number is given, it applies to all sizes. *Note: For ease in working, circle all numbers pertaining to the size you're making.*

FINISHED MEASUREMENTS

Underarm = 38 (42, 46, 49, 53, 56)"

YARN

Lion Brand Kool Wool (Art.380); 50% merino wool/50% acrylic; 1¾ oz. (50 g); 60 yds. (54 m); bulky weight

- 16 (17, 18, 19, 21, 23) balls #149 Charcoal

NEEDLES & EXTRAS

- Size 9 (5.5 mm) needles
- Size 9 (5.5 mm) 29" circular needle
- Size 10.5 (6.5 mm) needles *or size needed to obtain gauge*
- Stitch markers
- Stitch holders
- Blunt-end yarn needle
- Five ⅞" black buttons

GAUGE

15 sts and 18 rows = 4" (10 cm) over 1×6 Rib using larger needles.
TAKE TIME TO CHECK YOUR GAUGE.

PATTERN STITCHES

COMBINATION RIB

Row 1 (WS): P1; *k2, p2, k2, p1; rep from * across.

Row 2: K1; *p2, k2, p2, k1; rep from * across.

Rep Rows 1 and 2 for pat.

1×6 RIB

Row 1 (WS): P1; *k6, p1; rep from * across.

Row 2: K1; *p6, k1; rep from * across.

Rep Rows 1 and 2 for pat.

REVERSE STOCKINETTE STITCH (rev St st)

Row 1 (WS): Knit.

Row 2: Purl. Rep Rows 1 and 2 for pat. *Note: Work all decs and incs 1 st in from edge.*

INSTRUCTIONS

BACK

With smaller needles, cast on 72 (78, 86, 92, 100, 106) sts.

Foundation row (WS): P2 (0, 2, 0, 2, 0) sts, k2 (0, 2, 0, 2, 0) sts, work 64 (78, 78, 92, 92, 106) sts in Combination Rib, k2 (0, 2, 0, 2, 0) sts, p2 (0, 2, 0, 2, 0) sts. Work even in pat for 8 rows, ending with a RS row. Change to larger needles.

Setup row (WS): Work 4 (0, 4, 0, 4, 0) sts in Rev St st, work 64 (78, 78, 92, 92, 106) sts in 1×6 Rib, work 4 (0, 4, 0, 4, 0) sts Rev St st. Work even until piece measures 13¾ (14¼, 14¾, 15¼, 15¾, 16¼)", ending with a WS row.

Shape armholes: Bind off 8 (9, 9, 10, 11, 12) sts at beg of next 2 rows—56 (60, 68, 72, 78, 82) sts. Cont even until armhole measures 8¾ (9, 9, 9½, 9¾, 9¾)", ending with a WS row.

Shape shoulders and back neck: Work in pat across 20 (21, 25, 26, 29, 30) sts, join 2nd ball of yarn, bind off center 16 (18, 18, 20, 20, 22) sts for back neck, work in pat

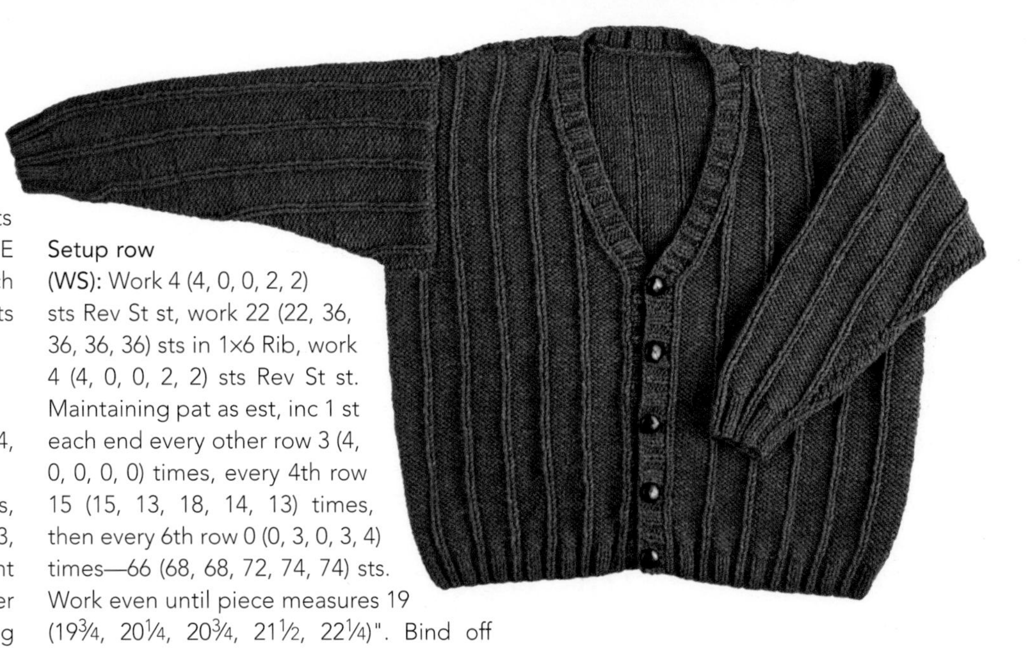

across rem 20 (21, 25, 26, 29, 30) sts. Working both sides at once, bind off 2 sts at each neck edge twice, and AT SAME TIME, bind off 6 (5, 7, 8, 9, 8) sts at each shoulder edge once, then 5 (6, 7, 7, 8, 9) sts twice—no sts rem.

RIGHT FRONT

With smaller needles, cast on 34 (37, 41, 44, 48, 51) sts.

Foundation row (WS): P2 (0, 2, 0, 2, 0) sts, k2 (0, 2, 0, 2, 0) sts, work 29 (36, 36, 43, 43, 50) sts in Combination Rib, k1 st (front edge). Keeping 1 st at front edge in Garter st (k every row), work even for 8 rows, ending with a RS row. Change to larger needles.

Setup row (WS): Work 4 (0, 4, 0, 4, 0) sts in Rev St st, work 29 (36, 36, 43, 43, 50) sts in 1×6 Rib, k1. Work even until piece measures same as Back to armhole, ending with a RS row.

Shape armhole: Bind off 8 (9, 9, 10, 11, 12) sts at beg of next row—26 (28, 32, 34, 37, 39) sts. Mark for beg of V-neck shaping.

Shape front neck—V-Neck Dec row: Work in pat to last 3 sts, ssk, k1. Rep V-Neck Dec Row along neck edge every other row 0 (2, 1, 2, 2, 3) times more, then every 4th row 9 (8, 9, 9, 9, 9) times—16 (17, 21, 22, 24, 26) sts. Work even until piece measures same as Back to shoulder shaping. Shape shoulders same as Back.

LEFT FRONT

With smaller needles, cast on 34 (37, 41, 44, 48, 51) sts.

Foundation row (WS): K1 st (front edge), work 29 (36, 36, 43, 43, 50) sts in Combination Rib, p2 (0, 2, 0, 2, 0) sts, k2 (0, 2, 0, 2, 0) sts. Work even for 8 rows, ending with a RS row. Change to larger needles.

Setup row (WS): K1 (front edge), work 29 (36, 36, 43, 43, 50) sts in 1×6 Rib, work 4 (0, 4, 0, 4, 0) sts in Rev St st.

Work to correspond to Right Front, reversing all shapings—V-Neck Dec row: K1, k2tog, work in pat to end.

SLEEVE (make 2)

With smaller needles, cast on 30 (30, 36, 36, 40, 40) sts.

Foundation row (WS): P2 (2, 0, 0, 0, 0) sts, k2 (2, 0, 0, 2, 2) sts, work 22 (22, 36, 36, 36, 36) sts in Combination Rib, k2 (2, 0, 0, 2, 2) sts, p2 (2, 0, 0, 0, 0) sts. Work even for 8 rows, ending with a RS row. Change to larger needles.

Setup row (WS): Work 4 (4, 0, 0, 2, 2) sts Rev St st, work 22 (22, 36, 36, 36, 36) sts in 1×6 Rib, work 4 (4, 0, 0, 2, 2) sts Rev St st. Maintaining pat as est, inc 1 st each end every other row 3 (4, 0, 0, 0, 0) times, every 4th row 15 (15, 13, 18, 14, 13) times, then every 6th row 0 (0, 3, 0, 3, 4) times—66 (68, 68, 72, 74, 74) sts. Work even until piece measures 19 (19¾, 20¼, 20¾, 21½, 22¼)". Bind off loosely in pat.

FINISHING

Sew Fronts to Back at shoulder seams.

Neckband: With RS facing, using smaller circular needle, and beg at bottom Right Front, pick up and k48 (50, 53, 54, 55, 57) sts along Right Front, place marker (pm), pick up and k1 st for V, pm, pick up and k37 (37, 38, 39, 41, 42) sts along right front neck, 28 (31, 30, 33, 34, 35) sts from back neck, 37 (37, 38, 39, 41, 42) sts along left front neck, pm, pick up and k1 st for V, pm, pick up and k48 (50, 53, 54, 55, 57) sts along Left Front—200 (207, 214, 221, 228, 235) sts.

Next row: Work Combination Rib, inc 1 st before and after marked V-neck sts—204 (211, 218, 225, 232, 239) sts. Mark position of 5 buttonholes evenly spaced on Left Front for men's version, Right Front for women's version. Cont in Combination Rib, working yo, k2tog buttonholes at marked positions on 4th row. Work Rib for 3 more rows. Bind off in pat. Sew 5 buttons to button band, positioning buttons according to buttonholes. Set in and sew Sleeves to body. Sew body and sleeve seams. Weave in all ends. Block lightly as necessary.

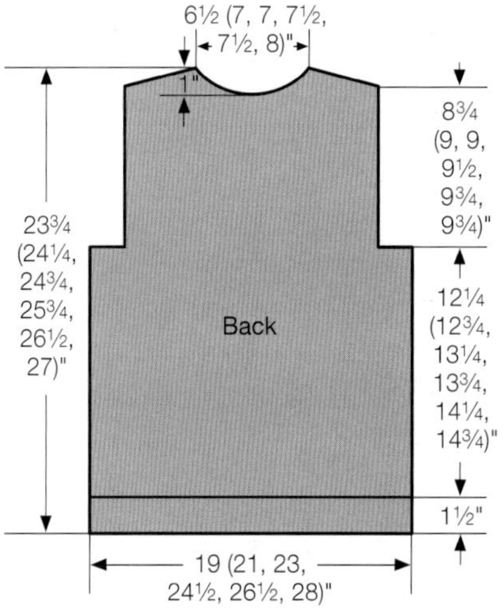

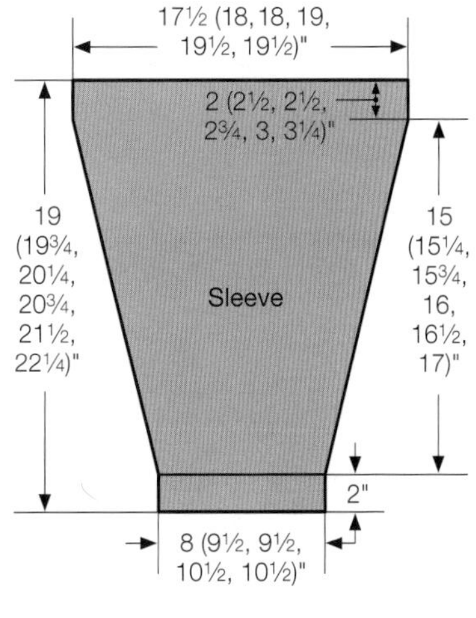

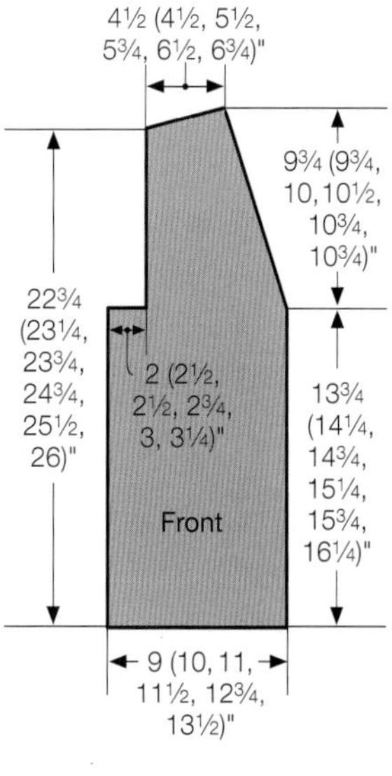

felted flower tote

Knit this terrific wool tote. Then run it through the washer and dryer! Its new, sturdy feel will last for seasons.

DESIGNER: LINDA W. CYR
PHOTOGRAPHER: PERRY STRUSE

SKILL LEVEL
Intermediate

FINISHED MEASUREMENTS
Before felting = approx $16\frac{1}{2}\times14\times4\frac{1}{2}$"
After felting = approx $16\times10\frac{1}{2}\times4\frac{1}{2}$"

Note: The tote will shrink more lengthwise than widthwise.

YARNS
Brown Sheep Lamb's Pride;
85% wool/15% mohair; 4 oz. (113 g);
125 yds. (114 m); bulky weight
- 4 skeins #M82 Blue Flannel (MC)

Brown Sheep Lamb's Pride;
85% wool/15% mohair; 4 oz. (113 g);
190 yds. (173 m); worsted weight
- 1 skein #M180 Ruby Red (A)
- 1 skein #M62 Amethyst (B)
- 1 skein #M155 Lemon Drop (C)
- 1 skein #M64 Turf Green (D)
- 1 skein #M41 Turkish Olive (E)

NEEDLES & EXTRAS
- Size $10\frac{1}{2}$ (7 mm) needles *or size needed to obtain gauge*
- Size $10\frac{1}{2}$ (7 mm) double-pointed needles (dpns)
- Size 8 (5 mm) needles
- Size 8 (5 mm) double-pointed needles (dpns)
- Size K (7 mm) crochet hook
- Blunt-end yarn needle
- Two 24" pieces of 1"-wide ribbon
- 1 sheet of stiff quilting template plastic (optional)

GAUGE
12 sts and 18 rows = 4" (10 cm) over St st (knit 1 row, purl 1 row) with bulky yarn on larger needles.
TAKE TIME TO CHECK YOUR GAUGE.

PATTERN STITCH
I-CORD
Row 1: Using dpns, k; do not turn.
Row 2: Slide sts to other end of needle. Knit.
Rep Row 2, forming a tube. Cont until desired length.

PARISIAN

INSTRUCTIONS

MAIN PIECE

With MC and larger needles, cast on 50 sts.
Work as follows: Work 1¼" of St st; 1½" of Garter st; 13" of St st; 4½" of Garter st; 13" of St st; 1¼" of Garter st; 1¼" of St st. Bind off all sts.

Note: The beg and end bands of St st are facings and will be used to help shape the tote during finishing.

RIGHT SIDE (AND POCKET)

With MC and larger needles, cast on 16 sts.
Work as follows: 1¼" of Garter st; 8¾" of St st; 13" of rev St st; 1¼" of Garter st. Bind off all sts.

LEFT SIDE

With MC and larger needles, cast on 16 sts.
Work as follows: 13" of St st; 1¼" of Garter st. Bind off all sts.

STRAP (make 2)

With 2 strands of E held tog and larger dpns, cast on 6 sts.
Work a 6-st I-Cord tube for 30". Cut yarn, leaving a 12" tail. Pull through sts and weave in end.

STEM (make 2)

With E and smaller dpns, cast on 4 sts.
Work a 4-st I-Cord tube for 36". Cut yarn, leaving a 12" tail. Pull through sts and weave in end.

LEAF (make 10)

With D and smaller needles, make a slip knot and place on left needle.
Row 1: [K1, p1, k1] in slip knot—3 sts.
Row 2 and all even rows: Purl.
Row 3: K1, M1, k1, M1, k1—5 sts.
Row 5: K2, M1, k1, M1, k2—7 sts.
Row 7: K3, M1, k1, M1, k3—9 sts.
Row 9: K4, M1, k1, M1, k4—11 sts.
Row 11: Knit.
Row 13: Ssk, k to last 2 sts, k2tog.
Row 15: Knit.
Rows 17, 19, and 21: Rep Row 13.
Row 23: Sl 1, k2tog, psso. Cut yarn, pull through sts, and weave in end.

FLOWER (make 2 each: A/C, C/B, B/A)

With A and smaller needles, cast on 6 sts.
***Row 1:** Inc in first st [k into front and back of st], k4, turn.
Row 2: P6, turn.
Rep last 2 rows 5 times more—12 sts.
Next row: Ssk, k5, turn.
Next row: P6, turn.
Rep last 2 rows 5 times more—6 sts.
Rep from * 4 times more.
Next row: Ssk, k4, turn.
Next row: P5.
****Next row:** Inc [k into front and back of st], k3, turn.
Next row: P5, turn. Rep last 2 rows 4 times more—10 sts.
Next row: Ssk, k4, turn.
Next row: P5, turn.
Rep last 2 rows 4 times more—5 sts.
Rep from ** 4 times more.
Next row: Ssk, k3, turn.
Next row: P4. Change to C.
*****Next row:** Inc [k into front and back of st], k2, turn.
Next row: P4, turn.
Rep last 2 rows 3 times more—8 sts.
Next row: Ssk, k3, turn.
Next row: P4, turn.
Rep last 2 rows 3 times more—4 sts.
Rep from *** 2 times more.
Bind off rem sts.

FINISHING

Fold 1¼" facings to inside of Main Piece; tack in place along bottom edge. Fold RS to create pocket; pin to Main Piece. With crochet hook and WS tog, work 1 row of sc to attach side. Work 1 row of sl st; fasten off. Rep to attach Left Side. Thread a piece of ribbon through each channel created by facings, tie ends tog at sides. Roll flowers into shape, letting each size of petal form a ring. Sew through all thicknesses of petals to hold tog. Cut all yarn ends, leaving 1" tails.

Felt the pieces by machine-washing in a Hot/Cold cycle with ¼ cup baking soda and drying in an automatic dryer on High. Remove ribbons. Steam-block the pieces. Using the photo as a guide, sew Straps in place. Arrange Stems and sew in place. Arrange Flowers and Leaves and sew in place. Cut two pieces of plastic 1" wide and 1" narrower than top of tote; round the ends. Insert plastic strips into channels. Sew channels closed, then sew tog at sides. If desired, cut a piece of quilting template plastic to fit bottom of tote; glue in place.

a simple twist

You'll love this all-in-one scarf and hat design!

DESIGNER: LIPP HOLMFELD
PHOTOGRAPHER: PERRY STRUSE

SKILL LEVEL
Beginner

FINISHED MEASUREMENTS
The scarf measures 11×48" before joining.

YARN
Lion Brand Imagine (Art. 780);
80% acrylic/20% mohair; 2½ oz. (70 g);
220 yds. (203 m); worsted weight
- 2 balls #114 Cerise

NEEDLES & EXTRA
- Size 10½ (6.5 mm) needles *or size needed to obtain gauge*
- Blunt-end yarn needle

GAUGE
18 sts and 16 rows = 4" (10 cm) over 1×1 rib.
TAKE TIME TO CHECK YOUR GAUGE.

PATTERN STITCH
1×1 RIB
Every row (on even number of sts): *K1, p1; rep from * across.

INSTRUCTIONS
Cast on 50 sts. Work every row in 1×1 Rib until strip measures 48". Bind off.

Bring ends of strip tog, forming a loop, then twist one end 180°. Using the blunt-end needle, join the ends.

To wear, place it over head around neck. Twist, then pull loop up and onto head.

faux-fur fun

Jazz up a denim shirt or jacket with these novelty attachments. Make the collar and cuffs separately, adjusting the length as needed, and tack in place.

DESIGNER: LINDA W. CYR PHOTOGRAPHERS: PERRY STRUSE, *OPPOSITE;* DEAN TANNER, *BELOW*

SKILL LEVEL
Easy

YARN
Lion Brand Fun Fur (Art. 320); 100% polyester; 1½ oz. (40 g); 57 yds. (52 m); medium weight
- 2 skeins #205 Sandstone

NEEDLES & EXTRAS
- Size 15 (10 mm) needles *or size needed to obtain gauge*
- Sewing needle
- Matching thread
- Denim shirt or jacket

GAUGE
10 sts and 20 rows = 4" (10 cm) in Garter stitch with double strand of yarn.
TAKE TIME TO CHECK YOUR GAUGE.

INSTRUCTIONS
***Note:** Collar and Cuffs are worked with two strands of yarn held together.*

COLLAR
Cast on 8 sts.
Work in Garter st until piece measures 18" (or same length as collar of garment); bind off.

CUFF (make 2)
Cast on 6 sts.
Work in Garter st until piece measures 11" (or same length as cuff of garment); bind off.

FINISHING
Sew pieces to shirt, overlapping each Cuff as needed.

half-pint hoodie

Here's a cutie! Make this quick jacket and learn how to graft stitches together to finish the hood.

DESIGNER: BONNIE EVANS PHOTOGRAPHER: PERRY STRUSE

SKILL LEVEL

Easy

SIZES

12 mos. (18 mos., 2T, 4T)

The pattern is written for the smallest size with changes for larger sizes in parentheses. When only one number is given, it applies to all sizes.

Notes: *For ease in working, circle all numbers pertaining to the size you're making. Use a double strand of yarn throughout.*

FINISHED MEASUREMENTS

Chest (buttoned) = 22 (24, 26, 28)"

Length = 11 (12½, 14, 15½)"

YARN

Lion Brand Microspun (Art. 910); 100% microfiber acrylic; 2½ oz. (70 g); 168 yds. (154 m); sport weight

- 3 (3, 4, 4) balls #194 Lime

NEEDLES & EXTRAS

- Size 5 (3.75 mm) knitting needles *or size needed to obtain gauge*
- Size 5 circular needle, 16" length
- One set of size 5 double-pointed knitting needles (dpns)
- Blunt-end yarn needle
- Ring-type stitch marker
- Five ¾"-diameter buttons in various colors
- Two stitch holders

GAUGE

In St st (knit 1 row, purl 1 row), 17 sts and 24 rows = 4" (10 cm).

TAKE TIME TO CHECK YOUR GAUGE.

Note: The cardigan is worked in one piece to the underarm.

SPECIAL TECHNIQUES

GRAFTING TWO STOCKINETTE PIECES TOGETHER

Hold the wrong sides together with the back and front needles pointed to the right. Thread the tail into the yarn needle. *Insert the needle knitwise through the first stitch on the front needle and let the stitch drop from the needle. Insert needle into the second stitch on the front needle purlwise and pull the yarn through, leaving the stitch on the needle. Insert the needle into the first stitch on the back needle purlwise and let it drop from the needle. Insert the needle knitwise through the second stitch on the back needle and pull the yarn through, leaving the stitch on the needle. Repeat from * across until all stitches have been joined. Adjust the tension as necessary. Weave in loose ends.

MAKE ONE STITCH (M1)

An increase made by lifting the horizontal thread lying between the needles and placing it onto the left needle. Knit into the back loop of this new stitch on the first row only.

INSTRUCTIONS

Using a double strand of yarn and beg at lower edge, cast on 98 (108, 116, 126) sts.

Rows 1–3: Knit.

BUTTONHOLE

Row 4 (WS): For girls, k to last 3 sts, yo, k2tog, k1. For boys, k1, yo, k2tog, k to end.

Eyelet rows—Row 5 (RS): K4; (yo, k2tog) across to last 4 sts, k4.

Row 6: K6; (yo, p2tog) across to last 4 sts, k4.

BODY PATTERN

Row 7 (RS): Knit.

Row 8: K4, p across to last 4 sts, k4.

Rows 9–38 (44, 50, 56): Rep Rows 7 and 8, adding a buttonhole on Row 20 (22, 24, 26) and then another on Row 36 (40, 44, 48)—on right band for girls and left band for boys. Add 1 more buttonhole after 15 (17, 19, 21) rows.

Shape armholes—Row 37 (41, 45, 49): K21 (24, 26, 28) sts and place these sts onto a holder for Right Front. Bind off 8 sts. K40 (44, 48, 54) sts and place onto a holder for Back. Bind off 8 sts. K rem 21 (24, 26, 28) sts.

LEFT FRONT

Beg with a WS row, k4, p17 (20, 22, 24) sts. Cont est pat, adding buttonhole for boys, until piece measures approx 10 (11½, 13, 14½)" from beg, ending with a RS row.

Shape neck: Bind off 4 sts kwise, p to end. K across, ending k2tog. P2tog, p to end.

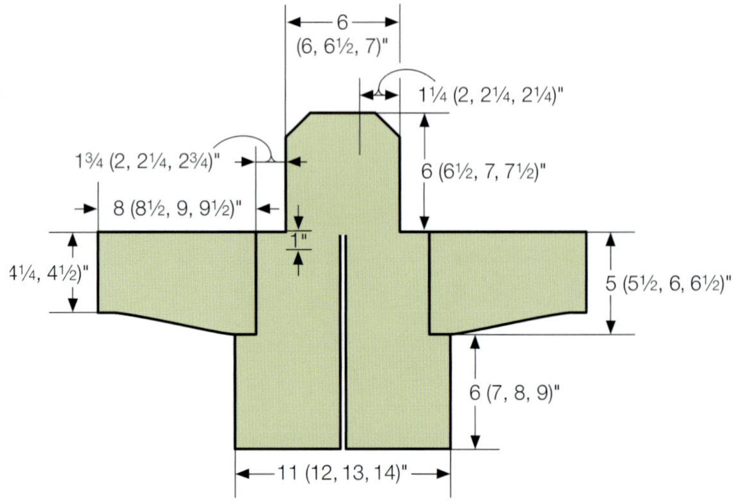

Cont in St st until front measures approx 11 (12½, 14, 15½)" from beg, ending with a WS row.

Place rem 15 (18, 20, 22) sts onto dpn. Cut yarn, leaving a 12" tail.

RIGHT FRONT

With WS facing, join yarn at armhole edge of Right Front. P17 (20, 22, 24) sts, k4.

Cont est pat, adding buttonhole for girls, until piece measures approx 10 (11½, 13, 14½)" from beg, ending with a RS row.

Shape neck: Bind off 4 sts kwise, k to end. P across, ending p2tog. K2tog, k to end. Complete as for Left Front.

BACK

With WS facing, join yarn and p40 (44, 48, 54). Work St st until Back measures approx 11 (12½, 14, 15½)" from beg, ending with RS row.

SHOULDER (make 2)

Refer to Grafting instructions on page 15. Beg at shoulder edge, join first 7 (9, 10, 12) sts for shoulder seam. Rep for 2nd side. With RS facing, return rem 42 (44, 48, 50) sts to one needle; join yarn at right neck edge.

HOOD

Row 1 (RS): K20 (21, 23, 24), M1, k2, M1, k to end—44 (46, 50, 52) sts.

Row 2: Purl.

Row 3: K21 (22, 24, 25), M1, k2, M1, k to end—46 (48, 52, 54) sts.

Row 4: Purl.

Cont inc in this manner for 5 more times—56 (58, 62, 64) sts. Work even in St st until Hood measures approx 8 (8½, 9, 9½)" from Shoulder, ending with a WS row. K28 (29, 31, 32) sts; cut yarn, leaving a 24" tail. Graft sts tog.

RIBBING

With RS facing, pick up and k65 (69, 73, 77) sts evenly spaced from corner of right front band, around Hood, ending at corner of left front band.

Row 1 (WS): P1; (k1, p1) across.

BUTTONHOLE

Row 2: For girls, k1, p1, yo, p2tog; (k1, p1) to end. For boys, (k1, p1) to last 4 sts, k2tog, yo, p1, k1.

Row 3: Rep Row 1.

Row 4: Bind off loosely in Ribbing.

SLEEVE (make 2)

With RS facing and using circular needle, pick up and k44 (48, 50, 54) sts evenly spaced around armhole, excluding the 8 bound-off sts. Beg with a p row, work 8 rows of St st. Distribute sts onto 3 dpn. Place a marker to indicate beg of rnd. Join and k every rnd for St st until Sleeve measures approx 7 (7½, 8, 8½)" from beg. At the same time, dec as follows:

Rnd 1: K1, k2tog, k to last 3 sts, k2tog, k1—42 (46, 48, 52) sts.

Rnds 2–7: Knit.

Rnd 8: Rep Rnd 1—40 (44, 46, 50) sts.

Rnds 9–12: Knit.

Rep Rnds 8–12 until 32 (34, 36, 38) sts rem.

EYELET ROUNDS

Rnd 1: K1; (yo, k2tog) around, ending k1.

Rnd 2: (Yo, k2tog) around.

GARTER-STITCH CUFF

Rnd 1: Purl.

Rnd 2: Knit.

Rnds 3 and 4: Rep Rnds 1 and 2.

Rnd 5: Bind off loosely and pwise.

FINISHING

Join underarm seams, sewing sleeve sides to the bound-off stitches at underarm for square armholes. Sew buttons opposite the buttonholes.

In search of a challenge? Capable knitters will find it in these fabulous Fair Isle and cable accessories.

snow-pretty trio

DESIGNER: GAYLE BUNN
PHOTOGRAPHERS: SCOTT LITTLE, *PAGES 18 AND 19*; ANDY LYONS, *PAGE 17*

SKILL LEVEL
Experienced

SIZE
Hat and Gloves: One size fits most adults.

FINISHED MEASUREMENTS
Scarf = approx 8x62"

YARNS
Patons Decor; 75% acrylic/25% wool; 210 yds. (194 m); worsted weight

For Hat and Gloves:
- 1 skein #1647 Burgundy (MC) MULTI
- 1 skein #1657 Claret (A) BLUE
- 1 skein #1662 Rich Bronze (B) GREEN
- 1 skein #1651 Coralberry* (C) WHITE
- 1 skein #1612 Rich Aqua* (D) MULTI

For Scarf:
- 3 skeins #1647 Burgundy

**As we went to press, Coralberry and Rich Aqua had been discontinued. Please substitute similar colors.*

NEEDLES & EXTRAS
- Size 3 (3.25 mm) set of double-pointed needles (dpns) for Gloves *or size needed to obtain gauge*
- Size 7 (4.5 mm) knitting needles for Hat and Scarf *or size needed to obtain gauge*
- Cable needle
- Blunt-end yarn needle
- Stitch marker

GAUGE
Hat and Scarf: In St st on size 7 needles, 20 sts and 26 rows = 4" (10 cm).
Gloves: In St st on size 3 needles, 24 sts and 32 rows = 4" (10 cm).
TAKE TIME TO CHECK YOUR GAUGE.

SPECIAL ABBREVIATIONS
Cr5B: Sl next 3 sts onto cable needle (cn) and leave at back of work. K2, then p1 from cn; k2 rem sts on cn.
T3B: Sl next st onto cable needle (cn) and leave at back of work. K2 then p1 from cn.
T3F: Sl next 2 sts onto cable needle (cn) and leave at front of work. P1, then k2 from cn.
MB: (K1, yo, k1, yo, k1) all in next st. Turn; p5. Turn; ssk, k1, k2tog. Turn; p3. Turn; sl 1, k2tog, psso—1 st rem. Bobble complete.
Ssk (sl, sl, k): Sl next 2 sts kwise, one at a time to right needle; insert tip of left needle into fronts of these 2 sts and k them tog.

PATTERN STITCH
CABLE PANEL (worked over 11 sts; a rep of 22 rows)
Row 1 (WS): K3, p2, k1, p2, k3.
Row 2: P3, Cr5B, p3.
Row 3: Rep Row 1.
Row 4: P2, T3B, p1, T3F, p2.
Row 5: K2, p2, k3, p2, k2.
Row 6: P1, T3B, p3, T3F, p1.
Row 7: K1, p2, k5, p2, k1.
Row 8: P1, k2, p5, k2, p1.
Rows 9 and 10: Rep Rows 7 and 8.
Row 11: Rep Row 7.
Row 12: P1, T3F, p3, T3B, p1.
Row 13: Rep Row 5.
Row 14: P2, T3F, p1, T3B, p2.
Row 15: Rep Row 1.
Row 16: Rep Row 2.
Row 17: Rep Row 1.
Row 18: Rep Row 4.
Row 19: Rep Row 5.
Row 20: P2, k2, p1, MB, p1, k2, p2.
Row 21: Rep Row 5.
Row 22: Rep Row 14.
Rows 1–22 form Cable Panel.

INSTRUCTIONS
SCARF
With MC and size 7 needles, cast on 38 sts. Work 9 rows in Garter St (k every row), noting first row is WS.
Row 10 (RS): K across, inc 7 sts evenly—45 sts.
Proceed in pat as follows:
Row 1 (WS): K3, work Row 1 of Cable Panel across next 11 sts, k3, work Row 19 of Cable Panel across next 11 sts, k3, work Row 1 of Cable Panel across next 11 sts, k3.
Row 2: K3, work Row 2 of Cable Panel across next 11 sts, p3, work Row 20 of Cable Panel across next 11 sts, p3, work Row 2 of Cable Panel across next 11 sts, k3.
Cable Panels are now in position. Cont in pat until Scarf measures approx 60", ending on Row 2 of Cable Panel for Outer Panels and Row 20 of Cable Panel for Center Panel.
Next row (WS): Knit, dec 7 sts evenly across—38 sts. Work 9 rows Garter st. Bind off kwise (WS).

GLOVES
RIGHT GLOVE
****Cuff:** With MC and size 3 needles, cast on 36 sts. Divide into 12 sts on 3 needles. Place marker to indicate beg of rnd; join.
Rnd 1: Knit.
Rnd 2: Purl.
Rnds 3–8: Rep last 2 rnds 3 times more.
Rnd 9: K 1 rnd, inc 4 sts evenly around—40 sts.
Rnds 10 and 11: With A, k.
Rnd 12: *With A, k1; with C, k1. Rep from * around. (This begins Fair Isle pat.)
Rnd 13: With C, k.
Rnd 14: With A, k.
Rnd 15: *With B, k1; with MC, k1. Rep from * around.
Rnd 16: With MC, k.
Rnd 17: *With MC, k1; with B, k1. Rep from * around.
Rnd 18: With A, k.
Rnd 19: With D, k.
Rnd 20: *With D, k1; with C, k1. Rep from * around.
Rnd 21: With D, k.
Rnds 22 and 23: With A, k. Cont with A for remainder of Glove.

Shape thumb gusset—Rnd 1: P1, (inc 1 st in next st) twice, p1, k to end of rnd.
Rnds 2–5: K all k sts and p all p sts as they appear.
Rnd 6: P1, inc 1 st in next st. K to 2 sts before the next p st, inc 1 st in next st, k1, p1, k to end of rnd.
Rnds 7 and 8: K all k sts and p all p sts as they appear.
Rep last 3 rnds until there are 12 sts bet the 2 p sts—50 sts. Work 2 rnds even.
Next rnd: Cast on 4 sts. Sl next 14 sts onto a thread for thumb. K to end of rnd—40 sts. K 9 rnds**.

Shape first finger: K first 4 sts. Sl all but last 8 sts onto a thread. Turn. Cast on 2 sts. Turn. K last 8 sts. Divide these 14 sts onto 3 needles. Join in rnd. K 20 rnds.
***Next rnd:** (K2, k2tog) 3 times, k2.
Next rnd: (K1, k2tog) 3 times, k2.
Next rnd: (K2tog) 4 times.
Break yarn. Thread end through rem 4 sts. Draw up and fasten securely*.

Shape second finger: Sl next 5 sts from thread. Turn. Cast on 2 sts. Turn. K last 5 sts. Pick up and k 2 sts at base of first finger. Divide these 14 sts onto 3 needles. K 22 rnds. Work from * to * as given for first finger.

Shape third finger: Sl next 5 sts from thread. Turn. Cast on 2 sts. Turn. K last 5 sts. Pick up and k 2 sts at base of second finger. Divide these 14 sts onto 3 needles. K 20 rnds. Work from * to * as given for first finger.

Shape fourth finger: Sl last 8 sts from thread. Pick up and k 2 sts at base of third finger. Divide these 10 sts onto 3 needles. K 16 rnds.
Next rnd: (K2tog) 5 times.
Next rnd: (K2tog) twice, k1.
Break yarn. Thread end through rem 3 sts. Draw up and fasten securely.

Shape thumb: K last 14 sts for thumb. Pick up and k 4 sts at base of thumb. Divide these 18 sts onto 3 needles. K 16 rnds.
Next rnd: (K4, k2tog) 3 times.
Next rnd: (K3, k2tog) 3 times.
Next rnd: (K2, k2tog) 3 times.
Break yarn. Thread end through rem 9 sts. Draw up and fasten securely.

LEFT GLOVE
Work from ** to ** as given for Right Glove.

Shape first finger: K first 8 sts. Sl all but last 4 sts onto a thread. Turn. Cast on 2 sts. Turn. K last 4 sts. Divide these 14 sts onto 3 needles. Join in rnd. K 20 rnds.
Work remainder of Left Glove to match Right Glove.

HAT

Edging (worked sideways): With MC and size 7 needles, cast on 17 sts.
Row 1 (WS): K3, work Row 1 of Cable Panel across next 11 sts, k3.
Row 2: K3, work Row 2 of Cable Panel across next 11 sts, k3.
Cable Panel is now in position. Cont in pat until edging measures approx 19½", ending with Row 3 of Cable Panel. Bind off in pat.
With RS of edging facing and MC, pick up and k 97 sts evenly across one long side of edging. With MC, k 1 row on WS for Garter st border. With A, k 1 row, p 1 row.
Proceed in Fair Isle pat as follows:
Row 1: With A, k1. *With MC, k2; with A, k2. Rep from * to end of row.
Row 2: With A, p.
Row 3: With B, k1. *With A, k2; with B, k2. Rep from * to end of row.
Row 4: With A, p.
Row 5: Rep Row 1.

MC - multi
A - [illegible]
B - [illegible]
C - [illegible]
D - multi

Row 6: With A, p.
Row 7: With A, k.
Row 8: *With A, p1; with C, p1. Rep from * to last st; with A, p1.
Row 9: With C, k1; *k2tog, k6. Rep from * to end of row—85 sts.
Row 10: With A, p.
Row 11: *With MC, k1; with B, k1. Rep from * to last st; with MC, k1.
Row 12: With MC, p.
Row 13: *With B, k1; with MC, k2tog, (with B, k1; with MC, k1) twice. Rep from * to last st; with B, k1—73 sts.
Row 14: With A, p.
Row 15: With D, k.
Row 16: *With C, p1; with D, p1. Rep from * to last st; with C, p1.
Row 17: With D, k1; *k2tog, k4. Rep from * to end of row—61 sts.
Row 18: With A, p.
Row 19: Rep Row 11.
Row 20: With MC, p.
Row 21: *With B, k1; with MC, k2tog; with B, k1; with MC, k1. Rep from * to last st; with B, k1—49 sts.
Row 22: With A, p.
Row 23: With D, k.
Row 24: Rep Row 16.
Row 25: With D, k1, *k2tog, k2. Rep from * to end of row—37 sts.
Row 26: With A, p.
Row 27: Rep Row 11.
Row 28: With MC, p.
Row 29: *With B, k1; with MC, k2tog. Rep from * to last st; with B, k1—25 sts.
Row 30: With A, p.
Row 31: With D, k1, *k2tog. Rep from * to end of row—13 sts.
Row 32: Rep Row 16.
Row 33: With D, k1, (k2tog) 6 times. Break yarn, leaving a long end. Draw end through rem 7 sts and fasten securely. Sew center back seam.

felted slippers

These slippers knit up huge. Felting brings them down to size.

DESIGNER: LINDA W. CYR
PHOTOGRAPHER: PERRY STRUSE

SKILL LEVEL

Easy

SIZES

S (M, L, 1X) to fit women's shoe sizes 5/6 (7/8, 9/10, 11/12)

Shown in Size S. The pattern is written for the smallest size with changes for larger sizes in parentheses. When only one number is given, it applies to all sizes.

Notes: For ease in working, circle all numbers pertaining to the size you're making. The slippers must be knit with a wool yarn—or in this case, a wool-and-mohair yarn—that hasn't been treated for machine washing.

FINISHED MEASUREMENTS

Length = 10 (11, 12, 13)"

YARNS

Brown Sheep Lamb's Pride Bulky; 85% wool/15% mohair; 4 oz. (113 g); 125 yds. (114 m); bulky weight

- 2 skeins #M65 Sapphire (MC)
- 1 skein #M120 Limeade (CC)

NEEDLES & EXTRA

- Size 11 (8 mm) needles *or size needed to obtain gauge*
- Nonskid liquid or spray (optional)

GAUGE

11 sts and 15 rows = 4" (10 cm) over St st (knit 1 row, purl 1 row) before felting.

Note: The slipper top is worked flat, then seamed along the top and back. The sole is worked back and forth from the outside in, then seamed down the center and sewn onto the bottom of the slipper top.

INSTRUCTIONS

TOP (make 2)

With MC, leaving a 15" tail, cast on 34 (36, 38, 42) sts.

Row 1 (RS): Sl 1 pwise, k across.

Row 2: Sl 1 pwise, k2, p to last 3 sts, k3.

Rep last 2 rows 12 (13, 15, 17) times.

Next row: Knit.

Next row: K2, p to last 2 sts, k2.

Work 12 (14, 16, 18) rows in St st (k on RS, p on WS).

Next row: K7, k2tog, ssk, k12 (14, 16, 20), k2tog, ssk, k7—30 (32, 34, 38) sts.

Work 3 (3, 5, 5) rows even in St st.

Next row: K6, k2tog, ssk, k10 (12, 14, 18), k2tog, ssk, k6—26 (28, 30, 34) sts.

Work 3 rows even in St st.

Next row: K5, k2tog, ssk, k8 (10, 12, 16), k2tog, ssk, k5—22 (24, 26, 30) sts.

Next row: Purl.

Next row: K4, k2tog, ssk, k6 (8, 10, 14), k2tog, ssk, k4—18 (20, 22, 26) sts.

Next row: Purl.

Bind off all sts. Cut yarn, leaving a 15" tail; fasten off.

Toe and Top Seam: Using the tail, gather the toe sts, then sew sides tog from toe to the beginning of Garter edging. Weave in ends.

Back Heel: Fold cast-on edge in half and sew tog using the tail. Fold bottom of back heel seam (i.e., the fold of cast-on edge) up to a point approx one-third of the seam length from the top edge; tack in place.

SOLE (make 2)

With CC, cast on 67 (75, 85, 93) sts.

Rows 1, 3, 6, and 8: Knit.

Row 2: Purl.

Row 4: *Pick up the st from cast-on edge that corresponds with next st on needle and place on left needle, k this tog with the next st; rep from * across, letting work curl to form a tube.

Row 5: [K1, k2tog] 2 (2, 3, 3) times; k13 (17, 15, 19); [k2tog, k2] 3 (3, 4, 4) times; k2tog, k1; [ssk, k2] 3 (3, 4, 4) times; ssk, k13 (17, 15, 19); [ssk, k1] 2 (2, 3, 3) times—55 (63, 69, 77) sts.

Row 7: K1; [k2tog] 2 (2, 3, 3) times; k12 (16, 13, 17); [k2tog, k2] 2 (2, 3, 3) times; k2tog, k1; [ssk, k2] 2 (2, 3, 3) times; ssk, k12 (16, 13, 17); [ssk] 2 (2, 3, 3) times; k1—45 (53, 55, 63) sts.

Sizes L and 1X only—Next row: K1, [k2tog] twice, k12 (16); [k2tog, k2] twice; k2tog, k1; [ssk, k2] twice; ssk, k12 (16), [ssk] twice, k1—45 (53) sts.

Next row: Knit.

All Sizes—Last row: K1, k2tog, k14 (18, 14, 18); [k2tog, k1] twice; [ssk, k1] twice; k8 (10, 8, 10), turn; k25 (29, 25, 29), turn; k10 (12, 10, 12), k2tog, k1, ssk, k15 (19, 15, 19), ssk, k1—37 (45, 37, 45) sts. Bind off all sts. Cut yarn, leaving an 18" tail.

FINISHING

Fold sole in half and sew center bottom seam using tail. With CC, sew sole to top, stitching securely all around. When drawn together, toe should sit above sole.

BALL DECORATION (make 2)

With CC, cast on 5 sts. K 9 rows and bind off all sts. Weave ends around outside edge and draw into a ball, tie ends securely, and stuff ends into center. Weave in all loose ends.

FELTING

Put slippers and balls into washing machine. (You might want to put them in a mesh bag to keep the lint from dispersing.) Using low water level, run a hot/cold cycle. Put in a pair of jeans for extra agitation. After one cycle, check for size. Repeat as necessary (sample slipper required two cycles). When slippers are the desired size, remove, shape, and stuff with newspaper. Let dry thoroughly. Sew on ball decorations.

To make the slippers safe to wear on a smooth surface such as hardwood or tile, apply a nonskid liquid or spray to the bottom of each slipper; let dry.

rugged raglan

Mottled yarn, horizontal banding, and a "dot" pattern texture this classic raglan and keep it interesting.

DESIGNER: ANN E. SMITH   PHOTOGRAPHERS: SCOTT LITTLE, *PAGE 24;* ANDY LYONS, *OPPOSITE*

SIZES

SMALL (M, L, XL)

The pattern is written for the smallest size with changes for larger sizes in parentheses. When only one number is given, it applies to all sizes.

Note: For ease in working, circle all numbers pertaining to the size you're making.

FINISHED MEASUREMENTS

Chest = 40½ (43, 45½, 48)"

Length = 25 (26, 27¼, 28)"

YARNS

Lion Brand Wool-Ease Chunky (Art. 630); 86% acrylic/10% wool/4% viscose; 5 oz. (140 g); 153 yds. (140 m); bulky weight

- 2 (2, 3, 3) balls #402 Wheat (A)
- 3 (4, 4, 4) balls #187 Foliage* (B)
- 1 (1, 2, 2) ball(s) #127 Walnut (C)

**As we went to press, #187 Foliage had been discontinued. Substitute a similar yarn color.*

NEEDLES & EXTRAS

- Size 10½ (6.5 mm) 29" circular knitting needle *or size needed to obtain gauge*
- Size 9 (5.5 mm) double-pointed needles (dpns)
- Size 9 straight needles
- 10 ring-type stitch markers
- Blunt-end yarn needle

GAUGE

In Stockinette stitch (knit 1 row, purl 1 row) and color pat with larger needle, 13 sts and 19 rows = 4" (10 cm).

TAKE TIME TO CHECK YOUR GAUGE.

SPECIAL ABBREVIATION

M1: Lift running thread before next stitch onto left needle and knit in its back loop to make one stitch.

Note: This pullover is worked from the neck down, knitting every round for Stockinette stitch (St st). After dividing for the garment sections, the pieces are worked back and forth on the circular needle in St st (knit on right-side rows, purl on wrong-side rows).

INSTRUCTIONS

With dpns and A, cast on 56 (64, 64, 64) sts. Arrange onto 3 needles with 19 (21, 21, 21) sts on first and 2nd needles and 18 (22, 22, 22) sts on 3rd needle. Place a double marker (2 markers) to mark beg of rnd; join and work 5 rnds of k1, p1 ribbing.

Note: The double marker is in center of right sleeve and is not referred to in the following directions; slip it on every rnd.

BACK

Yoke Setup: With size 10½ needle, k3 (5, 4, 4), place marker (pm), k1, pm, k20 (20, 22, 22), pm, k1, pm, k6 (10, 8, 8), pm, k1, pm, k20 (20, 22, 22), pm, k1, pm, k3 (5, 4, 4).

Yoke Pat—Rnd 1: *K to marker, M1, sl marker, k1, sl marker, M1; rep from * 4 total times—64 (72, 72, 72) sts.

Rnd 2: K around, slipping markers.

Rep Rnds 1 and 2 until there are 240 (264, 272, 288) total sts. Cut yarn, leaving a tail to weave in later.

Dividing rnd: Removing markers as you work, sl first 27 (31, 31, 33) sts onto a strand of yarn for first half of right sleeve. Join C and with size 10½ needle, k across next 66 (70, 74, 78) sts for Back. Sl 54 (62, 62, 66) sts onto a strand of yarn for Sleeve. Sl 66 (70, 74, 78) sts onto a strand of yarn for Front. Sl last 27 (31, 31, 33) sts onto a strand of yarn for 2nd half of right sleeve. Working back and forth on Back sts only, p 1 row. Work 3 more St st rows with C. Change to B and work 3 St st rows.

Lower Body Pat—Row 1 (RS): *With B, k3, k1–A; rep from * across, ending with k2–B.

Row 2: With B, p.

Row 3: With B, k.

Row 4: Rep Row 2.

Row 5: With B, k1; *k1–C, k3–B; rep from * across, ending with k1–C, k4–B.

Rows 6–8: Rep Rows 2–4.

Rep Rows 1–8 until piece from top of C stripe measures approx 11½ (11½, 12½, 12½)", ending with Row 2 or Row 6.

With B, k across next row, dec 1 st—65 (69, 73, 77) sts. P 1 row.

Change to size 9 straight needles.

Ribbing (worked with B)—Row 1 (RS): K1; (p1, k1) across.
Row 2: P1; (k1, p1) across.
Rep Ribbing Rows 1 and 2 for 4 times more. Bind off in ribbing.

LEFT SLEEVE

With RS facing, return 54 (62, 62, 66) sts to size 10½ needle. Join C and k across. Work 4 more St st rows.
Change to B and work 3 St st rows. Work Lower Body Pat Rows 1 and 2 as for Back.
Cont in est pat, dec 1 st each edge on next row, then every 6th row 8 (1, 1, 2) time(s), every 4th row 0 (10, 10, 10) times.
Work even on 36 (38, 38, 40) sts to approx 14 (14½, 15, 15½)" from beg, ending with Row 4 or Row 8 and dec 1 st in last row—35 (37, 37, 39) sts.
Change to size 9 straight needles and work Ribbing as for Back.

FRONT

With RS facing, return 66 (70, 74, 78) sts to size 10½ needle. Join C and work 5 St st rows, beg with a k row. Change to B and work 3 St st rows. Complete as for Back, beg with Lower Body Pat.

RIGHT SLEEVE

Work as for Left Sleeve.

FINISHING

Using matching colors, join underarm and side seams. Weave in loose ends on WS.

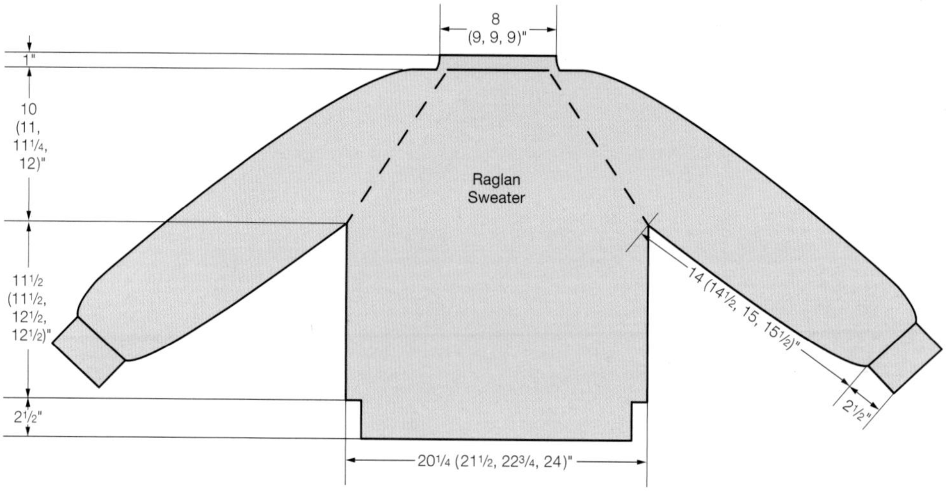

garden party

Sunny embroidery and touches of crochet set this top and purse abloom.

DESIGNER: LIPP HOLMFELD
PHOTOGRAPHERS: SCOTT LITTLE, *PAGE 27;*
ANDY LYONS, *THIS PAGE*

SKILL LEVEL
Intermediate

SIZES
Girls' 4 (6, 8, 10)
The pattern is written for the smallest size with changes for larger sizes in parentheses. When only one number is given, it applies to all sizes.
Note: For ease in working, circle all numbers pertaining to the size you are knitting before you begin.

FINISHED MEASUREMENTS
Chest = 24 (26, 28, 30)"
Length = 12½ (13½, 14½, 14½)"
Purse = Approx 6x7"

YARN
Patons Grace; 100% mercerized cotton; 1¾ oz. (50 g); 136 yds. (125 m); sport weight
- 4 (5, 5, 6) balls #60005 Snow

NEEDLES & EXTRAS
- Size 6 (4 mm) knitting needles *or size needed to obtain gauge*
- Size 5 (3.75 mm) knitting needles
- 11 daisy buttons
- DMC floss: 1 skein each of #327 Purple, #666 Red, #740 Orange, #743 Yellow, and #894 Pink
- Organza fabric for purse lining
- Size E/4 (3.5 mm) crochet hook
- Blunt-end yarn needle
- Sewing needle and white thread

GAUGE
In St st (knit 1 row, purl 1 row) with larger needles, 24 sts and 28 rows = 4" (10 cm). TAKE TIME TO CHECK YOUR GAUGE.

PATTERN STITCH
EYELET PATTERN
[a multiple of 8 sts + 8 (6, 12, 10) sts; a rep of 16 rows]
Row 1 (RS): K3 (2, 5, 4); * k2tog, yo, k6; rep from * across, ending last rep k2tog, yo, k3 (2, 5, 4).
Row 2: P all sts.
Row 3: Knit.
Rows 4–7: Alternately rep Rows 2 and 3.
Row 8: Rep Row 2.
Row 9 (RS): K7 (6, 9, 8); * k2tog, yo, k6; rep across, ending last rep k2tog, yo, k7 (6, 9, 8).
Rows 10–15: Alternately rep Rows 2 and 3.
Row 16: Rep Row 2.
Rep Rows 1–16 for Eyelet Pattern.

SWEATER
BACK—BORDER
Beg at lower edge, with smaller needles and MC, cast on 109 (114, 119, 124) sts. P 1 row. K 1 row.
Ruffle Rib—Row 1 (RS): P4; (k1, p4) across.
Row 2: K4; (p1, k4) across.
Rep last 2 rows to approx 2½" from beg ending with a RS row and dec 22 (21, 20, 19) sts evenly spaced across last row—87 (93, 99, 105) sts.
Gathering Rib—Row 1 (RS): K1; (p1, k1) across.
Row 2: P1; (k1, p1) across.
Rep last 2 rows to approx 3" from beg, ending with a RS row and dec 15 sts evenly spaced across last row—72 (78, 84, 90) sts.
Last Border: P 2 rows. K 2 rows. P 2 rows.

UPPER BODY
Change to larger needles. Beg with a p row, work St st until piece measures approx 7 (8, 8½, 8½)" from beg, ending with a RS row.
Shape armhole: Bind off 6 sts at beg of next 2 rows—60 (66, 72, 78) sts. Dec 1 st, every other row 5 times—50 (56, 62, 68) sts. Work even to approx 9½ (10½, 11, 11)" from beg, ending with WS row.
Keyhole Opening: K 25 (28, 31, 34) sts; join new strand and work to end of row. Work sides separately and at the same time to approx 11½ (12½, 13½, 13½)" from beg, ending with RS. Bind off 13 (14, 15, 16) sts at each neck edge; dec 1 st each neck edge once. Bind off rem 11 (13, 15, 17) sts for each shoulder.

FRONT
Work as for Back—Border.
Upper Body: Change to larger needles. Beg with a p row, work 7 St st rows. Beg Eyelet Pattern, working Rows 1–16. Cont est pat, shaping armholes as for Back. Work even to approx 11 (12, 13, 13)" from beg, ending with a WS row.
Shape neck: Work in pat across first 14 (16, 18, 20) sts; join new strand and bind off center 22 (24, 26, 28) sts; work to end of row. Working sides separately and at the same time, dec 1 st each neck edge, every other row 3 times. Work even on 11 (13, 15, 17) sts for each shoulder to approx 12½ (13½, 14½, 14½)" from beg, ending with a WS row. Bind off rem sts for each shoulder.

FINISHING
Join shoulder seams. Using the photo as a guide, embroider lazy-daisy stitches with floss around random eyelets.

Sew on 5 daisy buttons with the first at center of Last Border and the rem 4 spaced at 1½" intervals (2 on each side of center). Join side seams.

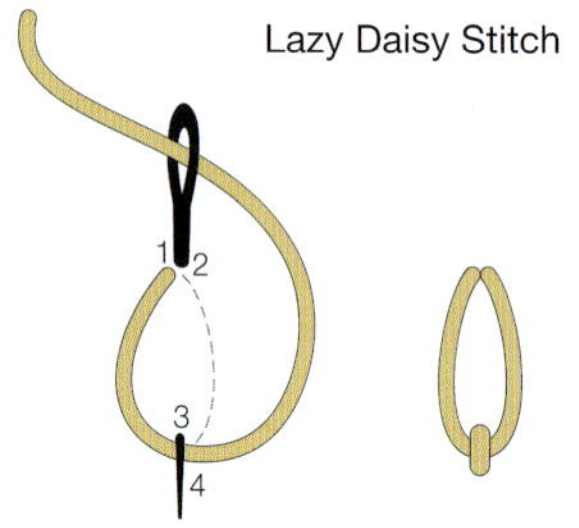

CROCHET EDGING
For armholes: With RS facing, join MC with a sl st at underarm. Ch 1, sc evenly around. At end, join with a sl st in first sc. Do not turn. Working from left to right rather than right to left, sc in each sc around (rev sc). At end, join and fasten off.
For neck: With RS facing, join MC with a slip st in corner of left back neck edge. Ch 1, sc evenly around to opposite neck edge; do not turn. Ch 1, working from left to right, sc in each sc around (rev sc). Fasten

off. With RS facing, join MC with a sl st ¾" from top of left back neck edge. Ch 7, sl st in corner and fasten off. Sew a daisy button to opposite edge. Weave in loose ends on WS of fabric. Without touching iron to fabric, lightly steam the garment.

PURSE

Beg at the top, with smaller needles and MC, cast on 44 sts. P 1 row. K 1 row.

Rep Ruffle Rib as for Back Border to approx 1¼" from beg, ending with RS row and dec 14 sts evenly spaced across last row—30 sts.

P 2 rows. K 2 rows. P 2 rows.

Beg with a p row, work 9 rows St st.

Eyelet Pattern—Row 1 (RS): K2; *k2tog, yo, k6; rep from * across, ending last rep k2tog, yo, k2.

Row 2: P all sts.

Row 3: Knit.

Rows 4–7: Alternately rep Rows 2 and 3.

Row 8: Rep Row 2.

Row 9: K6; *k2tog, yo, k6; rep from * across.

Rows 10–15: Alternately rep Rows 2 and 3.

Row 16: Rep Row 2.

Rep Rows 1–16 once more.

Rep Rows 1–8.

P 1 row on RS for turning ridge at base of Purse. Beg with a p row, work 7 St st rows. Rep Eyelet Pattern, Rows 1–16 once. Work 10 St st rows.

P 2 rows. K 2 rows. P 2 rows, inc 14 sts across last row—44 sts.

Rep Ruffle Rib for approx 1".

P 2 rows and bind off.

FINISHING

Using embroidery floss, work lazy daisy stitches around random eyelets.

Fold Purse in half along turning ridge. With RS facing and crochet hook, join MC with a sl st through both layers of fabric on lower edge. Ch 1, sc in same place as joining. Sc evenly along entire edge to join, leaving ruffle free.

At end, ch 50 for handle. Being careful to keep the ch untwisted, sc evenly along 2nd side to join. At end, turn. Ch 1, sc in each sc to the ch. *Ch 9, sk 9 ch, sl st in next ch; rep from * for 4 more times. Sc in each sc along first side and fasten off.

Sew 3 daisy buttons to each top edge of opening, placing one in the center and the others spaced ¾" on either side. Sew and attach a lining bag.

Without touching iron to fabric, lightly steam.

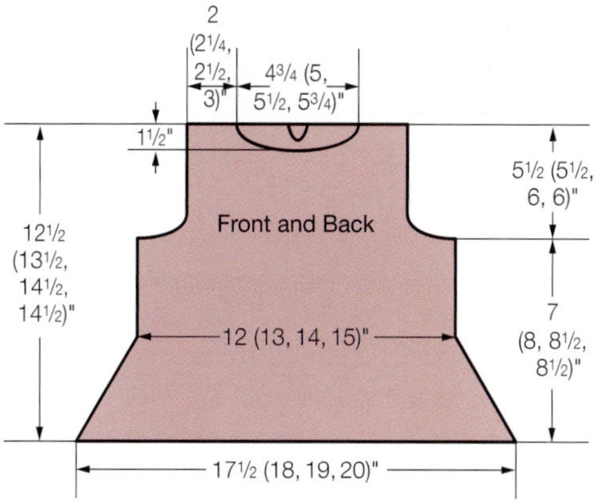

pom-pom treat

Knit this "suite" of I-cord stripes, pom-pom drops, and candy colors.

DESIGNER: DAWN OERTEL
PHOTOGRAPHERS: SCOTT LITTLE, *RIGHT;*
ANDY LYONS, *OPPOSITE*

SKILL LEVEL
Intermediate

FINISHED MEASUREMENTS
Approx 30×44", including trim

YARN
Wendy Velvet Touch; 100% nylon; 1¾ oz. (50 g); 115 yds. (105 m); sport weight
- 8 balls #1214 Pink (MC)

Patons Look At Me*; 60% acrylic/ 40% nylon; 152 yds. (139 m); sport weight
- 2 balls #6357 Hot Pink (A)
- 2 balls #6356 Mango (B)
- 2 balls #6383 Bright Lilac (C)
- 2 balls #6362 Green Apple (D)
- 1 ball #6366 Sunny Yellow (E)

**As we went to press, Patons Look At Me yarn had been discontinued. Substitute a suitable sport-weight yarn.*

NEEDLES & EXTRAS
- Size 6 (4.25 mm) circular knitting needle, 36" length, *or size needed to obtain gauge*
- Size 3 (3.25 mm) double-pointed needles (dpns)
- Pom-pom maker—1½" size
- Nine small stitch holders
- Blunt-end yarn needle

GAUGE
In Stockinette stitch (knit 1 row, purl 1 row) and color pat with size 6 knitting needle, 20 sts and 28 rows = 4" (10 cm).
TAKE TIME TO CHECK YOUR GAUGE.

Note: Use one ball of yarn for each vertical stripe. When changing color, bring next color from under present color for a twist to prevent holes.

INSTRUCTIONS
FIRST BORDER
I-cord: Using 2 dpns and A, cast on 5 sts. **Do not turn.* Slide sts to opposite end of needle and k5; rep from * to approx 3" from beg. *Do not cut yarn.* Place sts on holder. Make 8 more I-Cords as est in colors B, C, D, E, D, C, B, and A.

Setup Row: With size 6 needle, k5 I-cord A sts; *cast on 13 MC sts, k5 I-cord B sts; rep from * in color order listed above, ending cast on 13 MC sts, k5 I-cord A sts—149 sts.
Row 1: Purl across in est color pat. Rep Rows 1 and 2 on the 149 sts until piece measures approx 38" from Setup Row, ending with a WS row.

SECOND BORDER
Return 5 A sts to dpns and work as for beg I-cord Border for approx 3". Bind off. Pull tail into center of I-cord for easy finishing. Bind off MC stripe with larger needle. Rep as est for each I-cord and MC stripe across.

FINISHING
Wash throw in cold water and lay flat to dry. Make pom-poms in the following colors: 2 of A, 4 of B, 4 of C, 4 of D, and 4 of E. Attach a pom-pom to each I-cord as follows: A cord to C, B cord to D, C cord to E, D cord to B, and E cord to A.

Caution: Keep pom-pom fringe away from unattended babies and young children.

tumbling Ts crop top

Bursts of color set off this T-top, designed with square armholes and stockinette-stitch hems.

DESIGNER: LINDA W. CYR
PHOTOGRAPHER: ANDY LYONS

SKILL LEVEL

Easy

SIZES

S (M, L, XL)

The pattern is written for the smallest size with changes for larger sizes in parentheses. When only one number is given, it applies to all sizes.

Note: For ease in working, circle all numbers pertaining to the size you are knitting.

FINISHED MEASUREMENTS

Chest = 34½ (40½, 46½, 52½)"

Length = 18 (19, 20, 20½)"

YARNS

Classic Elite Yarn Sand*; 100% cotton; 77 yds. (70 m); worsted weight

- 6 (6, 7, 8) skeins #6485 Orange (A)
- 6 (6, 6, 7) skeins #6402 Gold (B)
- 6 (6, 6, 7) skeins #6493 Ultramarine (C)
- 5 (5, 5, 6) skeins #6434 Fuchsia (D)

**As we went to press, Sand had been discontinued. Please choose a substitute yarn in worsted weight and suitable colors.*

NEEDLES

- Size 8 (5 mm) knitting needles *or size needed to obtain gauge*
- Size 6 (4.25 mm) knitting needles
- Size 10 (6 mm) knitting needles
- Blunt-end yarn needle

GAUGE

In Geometric Pattern with size 8 needles, 16 sts and 26 rows = 4" (10 cm).

TAKE TIME TO CHECK YOUR GAUGE.

PATTERN STITCH

Geometric Pattern (a multiple of 12 sts + 9 sts; a rep of 16 rows): See chart.

Note: Use intarsia technique throughout; that is, use a separate strand for each color area. DO NOT CARRY UNUSED COLOR ALONG BACK OF WORK. When changing color, bring next color from under present color for a twist to prevent holes.

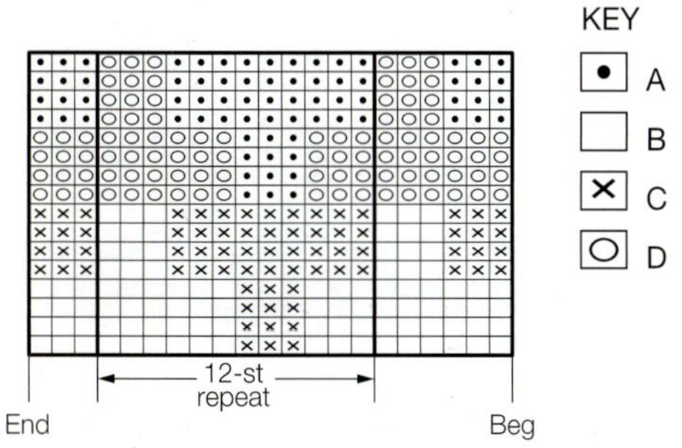

INSTRUCTIONS

BACK

Beg at lower edge with size 6 needles and A, cast on 62 (73, 84, 95) sts.

Hem Facing: Work St st to approx 1½" from beg, ending after WS row, inc 7 (8, 9, 10) sts evenly across last row—69 (81, 93, 105) sts.

Body Pat (Turning Row): Change to size 10 needles, and work Row 1 of Geometric Pat. Change to size 8 needles, cont in Geometric Pat, and work even to approx 8½ (9, 9½, 9½)" from Turning Row, ending after a WS row.

Shape armholes: Bind off 6 (6, 12, 12) sts at beg of next 2 rows—57 (69, 69, 81) sts. Work even to approx 17 (18, 19, 19½)" from Turning Row, ending after WS row.

Shape shoulders: Bind off 5 (7, 7, 9) sts at beg of next 6 rows. Bind off rem 27 sts.

FRONT

Work as for Back until piece measures approx 15½ (16½, 17½, 18)" from Turning Row, ending after Row 8 or Row 16 of pat.

Shape neck: Work in pat across first 21 (27, 27, 33) sts; sl center 15 sts onto holder; join new strands of yarn, and work to end of row. Work sides with separate balls of yarn, and bind off 2 sts each neck edge twice, then dec 1 st each neck edge every other row twice—15 (21, 21, 27) sts rem for each shoulder. Complete shoulders as for Back.

SLEEVE (make 2)

Beg at lower edge with size 6 needles and Color A, cast on 40 sts.

Hem Facing: Work St st to approx 1½" from beg, ending after WS row, inc 5 sts evenly across last row—45 sts.

Body Pat (Turning Row): Change to size 10 needles, and work Row 1 of Geometric Pat. Change to size 8 needles, and work even in Geometric Pat until piece measures approx 1½" from Turning Row. Beg with next RS row, including new sts into pat as they accumulate, inc at each edge every 4th row 0 (0, 0, 4) times, every 6th row 0 (4, 11, 14) times, every 8th row 5 (10, 5, 0) times, then every 10th row 7 (0, 0, 0) times—69 (73, 77, 81) sts. Work even to approx 21 (20, 20½, 19½)" from Turning Row, ending after WS row. Bind off.

FINISHING

Join left shoulder seam.

Neckband: With RS facing and size 8 needles, begin at back neck and pick up and k27 sts with correct colors.

With correct colors, pick up and k16 sts along side of neck, k15 sts from holder, and pick up and k16 sts along next side of neck—74 sts. Working back and forth, cont in Geometric Pat until band measures approx 2¼" from beg.

Next row: Change to size 10 needles, and work 1 more row in pat.

Next row: Change to size 6 needle, cont in St st with A only, and dec 8 sts evenly around—66 sts. Cont until band measures approx 5" from beg. Bind off very loosely. Sew left shoulder seam, including side of neckband. Loosely whipstitch facings at lower edges and neckline to WS of sweater. Set in sleeves, sewing bound-off sts to sleeve sides for square armholes. Sew sleeve and side seams.

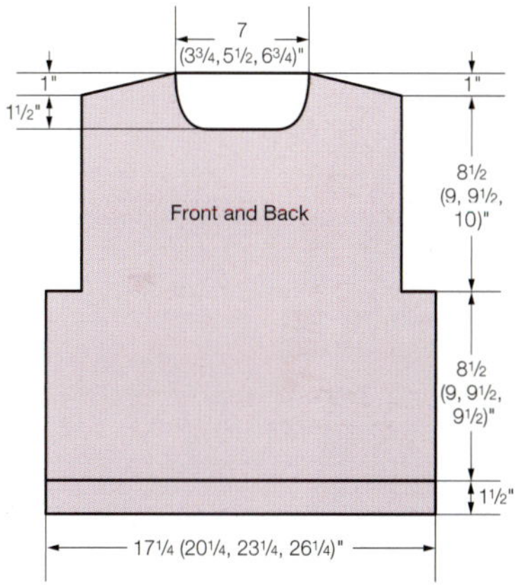

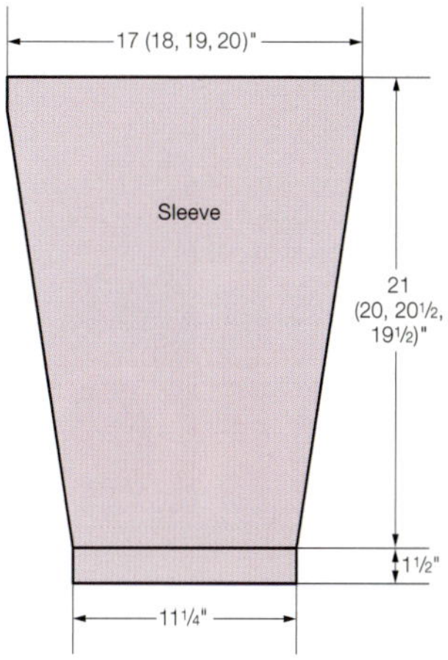

Sharp graphics set up this pillow threesome worked with bold colors and doubled yarn.

pillow symmetry

DESIGNER: VAL LOVE
PHOTOGRAPHERS: SCOTT LITTLE, *PAGES 33–35*; ANDY LYONS, *PAGE 32*

Nine-Patch Graphic

SKILL LEVEL
Easy

FINISHED MEASUREMENTS
Approx 12" square, plus a ¾" border

YARNS
Patons Grace; 100% mercerized cotton; 136 yds. (124 m); sport weight
- 4 balls #60011 Champagne (MC)
- 1 ball #60409 Ruby (A)
- 1 ball #60604 Terra-Cotta (B)

NEEDLES & EXTRAS
- Size 5 (3.75 mm) knitting needles *or size needed to obtain gauge*
- Blunt-end yarn needle
- 12"-square pillow form

GAUGE
In Stockinette stitch (knit 1 row, purl 1 row) with a double strand of yarn, 22 sts and 30 rows = 4" (10 cm).
TAKE TIME TO CHECK YOUR GAUGE.

Notes: Use two strands of yarn held together throughout this project to produce a fabriclike texture. Each square within the design is 22 stitches wide and 30 rows deep. Make a small ball of yarn, using two strands for each color. When starting a new color, tie the new color around the color in use with a slip knot. When changing yarn color within the design, twist the new color around the color in use.

INSTRUCTIONS

FRONT
Using a double strand of MC, cast on 74 sts. K 7 rows for Garter st border.

Body pat—Row 1 (RS): K4-MC; k22-A, k22-B, k22-A, k4-MC.

Row 2: K4-MC, p22-A, p22-B, p22-A, k4-MC.

Rows 3–30: Rep last 2 rows 14 times more.

Row 31: K4-MC, k22-B, k22-MC, k22-B, k4-MC.

Row 32: K4-MC, p22-B, p22-MC, p22-B, k4-MC.

Rows 33–60: Rep Rows 31 and 32 fourteen times more.

Rows 61–90: Rep Rows 1 and 2 fifteen times more.

With MC, k 7 rows for top border. With one strand only, bind off.

BACK
Using a double strand of MC, cast on 66 sts. Beg with a k row, work 90 rows of St st. Piece should measure approx 12" square. With one strand only, bind off.

FINISHING
Weave loose ends along WS of fabric, closing holes as necessary. Holding WS tog, place base of back next to Garter st border. Using 1 strand of yarn, sew 3 sides tog along inside edge of border (1 st per knitted st is best). Insert pillow form and sew rem side closed.

Bars and Blocks

SKILL LEVEL
Intermediate

FINISHED MEASUREMENTS
Approx 12" square, plus a ¾" border

YARNS
Patons Grace; 100% mercerized cotton; 136 yds. (124 m); sport weight

- 5 balls #60011 Champagne (MC)
- 1 ball #60040 Night (A)
- 1 ball #60005 Snow (B)

NEEDLES & EXTRAS
- Size 5 (3.75 mm) knitting needles *or size needed to obtain gauge*
- Blunt-end yarn needle
- 12"-square pillow form

GAUGE
In Stockinette stitch (knit 1 row, purl 1 row) with a double strand of yarn, 22 sts and 30 rows = 4" (10 cm).
TAKE TIME TO CHECK YOUR GAUGE.

PATTERN STITCH
SEED STITCH
Row 1 (WS): K1; (p1, k1) across.
Row 2: Knit the purl sts and purl the knit sts as they face you.
Rep Rows 1 and 2 for seed st.

Notes: Double strands of yarn are used for entire project. Each square within design is 13 stitches wide and 18 rows deep. Stripes are two rows deep. Make a small ball of yarn using two strands for each color. When starting a new color, tie new color around color in use with a slip knot. When changing yarn color within the design, twist the new color around the color in use.

INSTRUCTIONS
FRONT
Using a double strand of MC, cast on 73 sts. Work 5 rows of seed st.
First chart row (RS): With MC, work 4 seed sts; (k13-MC, k13-A) twice, k13-MC, with MC, work 4 seed sts. Pat is now set. Follow chart, *below*, through completion of Row 90. With MC, work 5 rows of seed st. Bind off, using a single strand of MC.

BACK
Using a double strand of MC, cast on 65 sts. Beg with a knit row, work 90 rows of St st. Piece should measure approx 12" square. Bind off using a single strand.

FINISHING
Weave loose ends along WS of fabric, closing holes as necessary. Holding WS tog, use a single strand of MC to join Back to base of border on 3 sides. Insert pillow form and sew rem side closed.

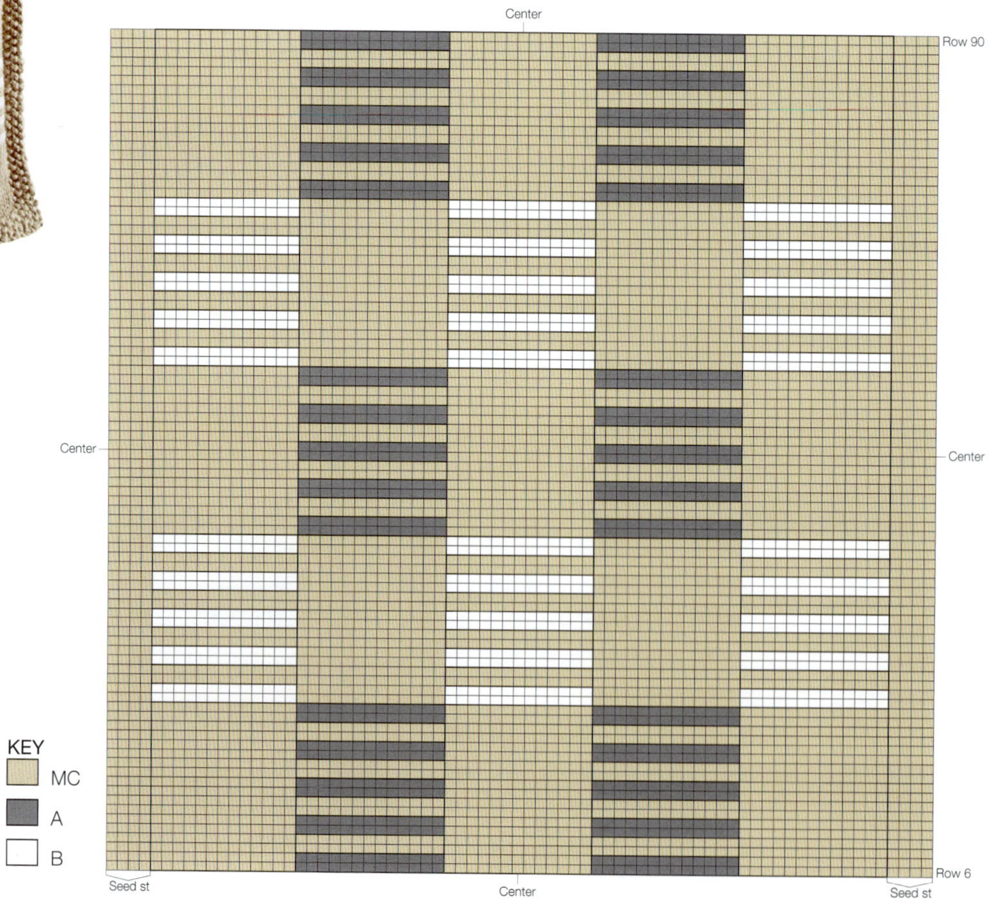

In-Line Design

SKILL LEVEL

Intermediate

FINISHED MEASUREMENTS

Approx 12" square

YARNS

Patons Grace; 100% mercerized cotton; 136 yds. (124 m); sport weight

- 5 balls #60040 Night (MC)
- 1 ball #60134 Royal (A)
- 1 ball #60712 Lime (B)
- 1 ball #60705 Cardinal (C)

NEEDLES & EXTRAS

- Size 5 (3.75 mm) knitting needles or *size needed to obtain gauge*
- Blunt-end yarn needle
- 12"-square pillow form

GAUGE

Using a double strand of yarn in Stockinette stitch (knit 1, purl 1), 22 sts and 30 rows = 4" (10 cm).
TAKE TIME TO CHECK YOUR GAUGE.

Notes: The pillow top is made in one piece using double strands of yarn throughout. Make a small ball of yarn using two strands for each color. When starting a new color, tie new color around color in use with a slip knot. When changing color within the design, twist the new color around the color in use.

INSTRUCTIONS

FRONT and BACK

Front and Back are worked as one piece. Using a double strand of MC, cast on 70 sts. Beg with a k row, work 5 St st rows.
First chart row 6 (WS): P25-MC, p20-A, p25-MC. (See chart, *below.*) Chart pat is now set. Follow chart through completion of Row 89. Beg with a purl row, work 5 St st rows with MC. Rep chart rows 6–89 once more. Beg with a purl row, work 5 St st rows with MC. Bind off with MC.

FINISHING

Fold pillow top in half with RS tog. Using a single strand of MC, sew sides tog through 2 thicknesses, 1 st in from each edge (1 st per knitted st is best). Weave loose ends along WS of fabric, closing holes as necessary. Turn RS out. Insert pillow form and sew rem side closed.

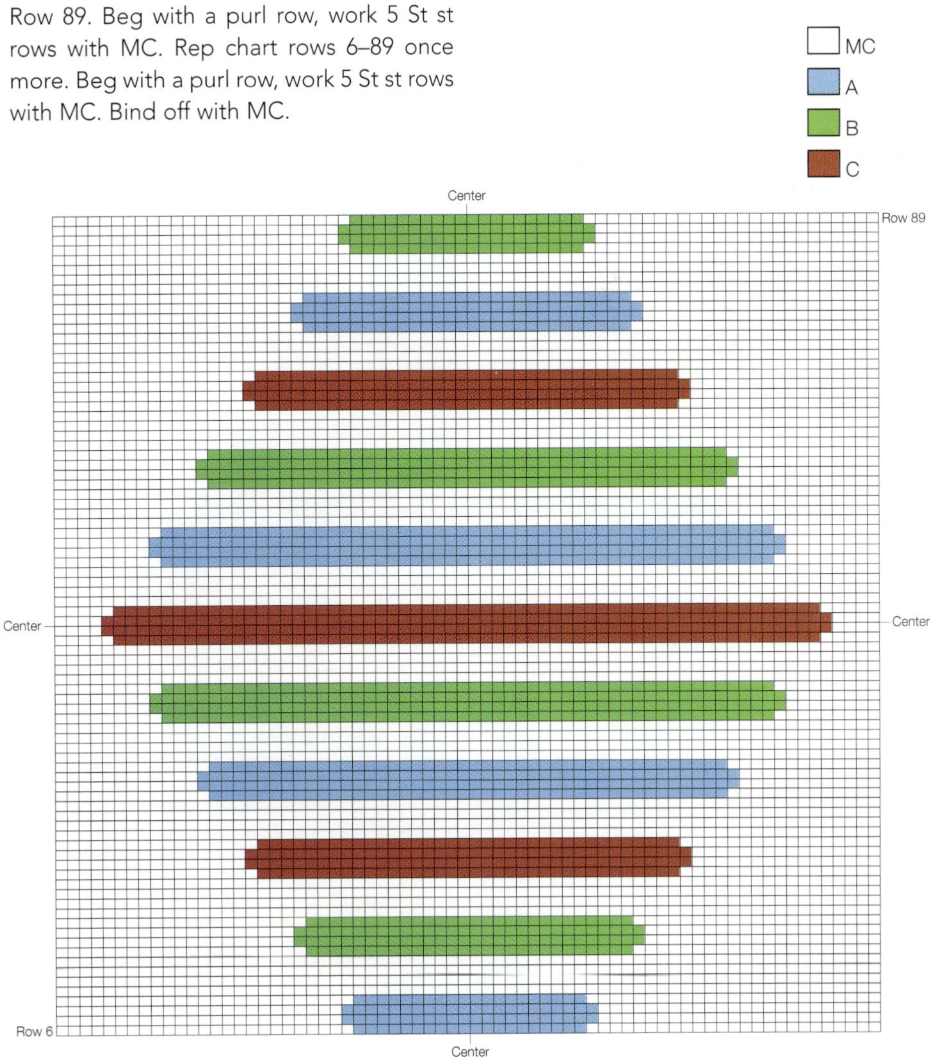

novelty stripe

Suitable for knitters with minimal experience, this cardigan is striped and textured with two different yarns.

DESIGNER: KRISTEN SLADE
PHOTOGRAPHER: PERRY STRUSE

SKILL LEVEL
Easy

SIZES
S (M, L, 1X, 2X)

Shown in Size S. The pattern is written for the smallest size with changes for larger sizes in parentheses. When only one number is given, it applies to all sizes.

Note: For ease in working, circle all numbers pertaining to the size you're making.

FINISHED MEASUREMENTS
Underarm (buttoned) = 36½ (39½, 43, 48, 53)"

YARNS
Lion Brand Homespun (Art. 790); 98% acrylic/2% polyester; 6 oz. (171 g); 185 yds. (167 m); bulky weight

- 3 (4, 5, 6, 6) skeins #362 Quartz (MC)

Lion Brand Fun Fur (Art. 320); 100% polyester; 1½ oz. (40 g); 57 yds. (52 m); bulky weight

- 3 (3, 4, 4, 4) skeins #208 Tropical (CC)

NEEDLES & EXTRAS
- Size 9 (5.5 mm) needles *or size needed to obtain gauge*
- Blunt-end yarn needle
- Five ⅞" buttons

GAUGE
13 sts and 20 rows = 4" (10 cm) over Stockinette stitch (knit 1 row, purl 1 row).
TAKE TIME TO CHECK YOUR GAUGE.

Note: Work all incs and decs one stitch (selvedge) in from edge. Work all selvedge stitches in St st (k on RS, p on WS).

PATTERN STITCH
STRIPE SEQUENCE

Rows 1 (RS) and 2: Work St st using MC.
Rows 3 and 4: Work Garter st using CC.
Rows 5 and 6: Work St st using MC.
Rows 7 and 8: Work Garter st using CC.
Rows 9–16: Work St st using MC.
Rep Rows 3–16 for Stripe Sequence.

INSTRUCTIONS
BACK

With MC, cast on 60 (66, 72, 80, 88) sts. Work in Garter st (k every row) for 6 rows. Work Stripe Sequence until piece measures 14½ (14½, 15, 15, 16)", ending with a WS row.

Shape armholes: Bind off 4 sts at beg of next 2 rows—52 (58, 64, 72, 80) sts. Cont in pat until piece measures 23½ (23½, 25, 25½, 26½)". Bind off loosely.

LEFT FRONT

With MC, cast on 28 (31, 34, 38, 42) sts. Work as for Back until piece measures 20 (20, 21½, 22, 23)", ending with a RS row—24 (27, 30, 34, 38) sts.

Shape neck: Bind off 3 (3, 4, 4, 5) sts at beg of next row—21 (24, 26, 30, 33) sts.

Dec Row (RS): Work to last 3 sts, k2tog, k1. Rep Dec Row every other row 4 (4, 4, 5, 5) times more—16 (19, 21, 24, 27) sts. Cont in pat until piece measures same as for Back. Bind off loosely.

RIGHT FRONT

Work as for Left Front until piece measures 20 (20, 21½, 22, 23)", ending with a WS row—24 (27, 30, 34, 38) sts.

Shape neck: Bind off 3 (3, 4, 4, 5) sts at beg of next row. Work 1 row even.

Dec Row (RS): K1, ssk, work to end. Rep Dec Row every other row 4 (4, 4, 5, 5) times more—16 (19, 21, 24, 27) sts. Cont in pat until piece measures same as for Back. Bind off loosely.

SLEEVE (make 2)

With MC, cast on 28 (28, 32, 32, 36) sts. K 6 rows. Work 4 rows St st.

Inc Row: K1 (selvedge), M1, work to last st, M1, k1 (selvedge st) [see Note under Gauge]. Cont in St st and rep Inc Row every 4th row 16 (16, 14, 14, 10) times and every 6th row 0 (0, 3, 5, 7) times—62 (62, 68, 72, 72) sts. Work even until piece measures 19 (19, 20, 20, 21)". Bind off loosely.

FINISHING

Sew fronts to Back at shoulders. Sew Sleeves to body. Sew side and underarm seams.

Button Band: With MC and RS facing, pick up and k58 (58, 62, 66, 70) sts along Left Front edge. K 6 rows. Bind off loosely.

Buttonhole Band: With MC and RS facing, pick up and k58 (58, 62, 66, 70) sts along Right Front edge. K 2 rows.

Buttonhole Row: K4, *yo, k2tog, k10 (10, 11, 12, 13); rep from * 3 more times; yo, k2tog, k4. K 3 rows. Bind off loosely.

Neckband: With CC and RS facing, pick up and k74 (74, 76, 76, 78) sts evenly along neck. K 3 rows. Bind off loosely. Weave in loose ends. Sew buttons opposite buttonholes.

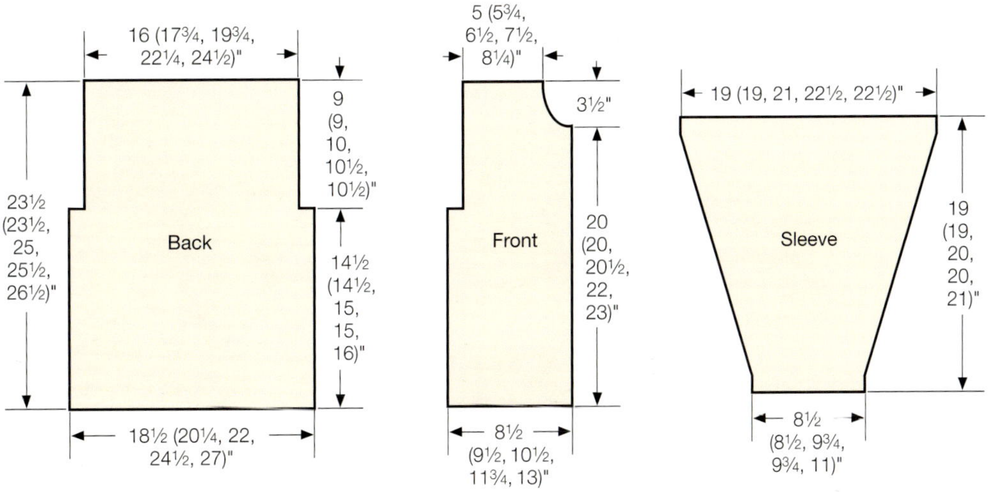

little lambs pullover

The fluffy lambs are knitted right into this sweet design.

DESIGNER: LISA CARNAHAN
PHOTOGRAPHER: PERRY STRUSE

SKILL LEVEL
Intermediate

SIZES
2 (4, 6, 8)
Shown in Size 4. The pattern is written for the smallest size with changes for larger sizes in parentheses. When only one number is given, it applies to all sizes.
Note: *For ease in working, circle all numbers pertaining to the size you're making.*

FINISHED MEASUREMENTS
Underarm = 28 (30, 32, 34)"

YARNS
Lion Brand Cotton-Ease (Art. 700); 50% cotton/50% acrylic; 3½ oz. (100 g); 207 yds. (188 m); worsted weight
- 1 (1, 1, 2) balls #169 Pistachio (A)
- 2 (2, 3, 3) balls #107 Candy Blue (B)
- 1 ball #153 Licorice (C)
- 1 ball #100 Vanilla (D)

Lion Brand Polarspun (Art. 360); 100% polyester; 1¾ oz. (50 g); 137 yds. (123 m); worsted weight
- 1 ball #100 Snow White (E)

NEEDLES & EXTRAS

- Size 7 (4.5 mm) needles
- Size 7 (4.5 mm) 16" circular needle
- Size 8 (5 mm) needles *or size needed to obtain gauge*
- Stitch holders
- Stitch marker
- Blunt-end yarn needle

GAUGE

18 sts and 26 rows = 4" (10 cm) with larger needles in Stockinette stitch (knit 1 row, purl 1 row).

TAKE TIME TO CHECK YOUR GAUGE.

PATTERN STITCH

FENCE

Row 1: With D, *k1, sl 3 (these will be A); rep from * to end.

Row 2: With D, *sl 3, p1; rep from * to end.

Rows 3, 7, and 11: With B, *sl 1 (this will be D); k3; rep from * to end.

Rows 4, 8, and 12: With B, *p3, sl 1; rep from * to end.

Rows 5, 6, 9, and 10: With D, knit.

Notes: Work all decs one stitch in from edge as follows: at beg of RS row, dec = ssk; at end of RS row, dec = k2tog; at beg of WS row, dec = p2tog; at end of WS row, dec = ssp (see Special Abbreviation, below.) Work first and last stitch in St st for selvedge. Inc row: K2, M1, k to last 2 sts, M1, k2.

SPECIAL ABBREVIATION

Ssp: Sl next 2 sts kwise; pass back to left needle. P2tog through back lps.

Note: When changing colors on Front, drop color in use, then bring 2nd color under and around first and cont knitting. This eliminates holes bet 2 colors.

INSTRUCTIONS

BACK

With smaller needles and A, cast on 64 (68, 72, 76) sts. Work in k1, p1 rib for 1", ending on a WS row. Change to larger needles and work in St st for 1", ending on a WS row.

Next row: With A, k5 (7, 9, 11), work Row 1 of Chart A; with A, k9; work Row 1 of Chart B; with A, k9; work Row 1 of Chart C; with A, k5 (7, 9, 11). Cont working charts as est in St st, ending with Row 18 of charts. With A, work 4 rows of St st, ending on WS. Work Fence Pattern until complete. With B, work even in St st until piece measures 8½ (9¼, 10, 10¾)" from beg, ending with a WS row.

Shape armholes: Bind off 5 sts at beg of next 2 rows—54 (58, 62, 66) sts. Work even until armhole measures 4½ (4¾, 5, 5¼)", ending with a WS row.

Shape back of neck: Work 20 (21, 22, 23) sts, place center 14 (16, 18, 20) sts on holder for Back neck, attach another ball of yarn and work remaining 20 (21, 22, 23) sts. Working both sides at same time, work in St st and dec 1 st at each neck edge 3 times [see Notes under Pattern Stitch]—17 (18, 19, 20) sts. Work even until armhole measures 5½ (5¾, 6, 6¼)". Place sts on holders for shoulders.

FRONT

Work as for Back until armhole measures 3½ (3¾, 4, 4¼)".

Shape front of neck: Work 23 (24, 25, 26) sts, place center 8 (10, 12, 14) sts on holder for neck, attach another ball of yarn and work remaining 23 (24, 25, 26) sts. Working both sides at same time, work in St st and bind off 2 sts on each neck edge 1 time, then dec 1 st on each neck edge every row 4 times [see Notes under Pattern Stitch]—17 (18, 19, 20) sts. Work even until

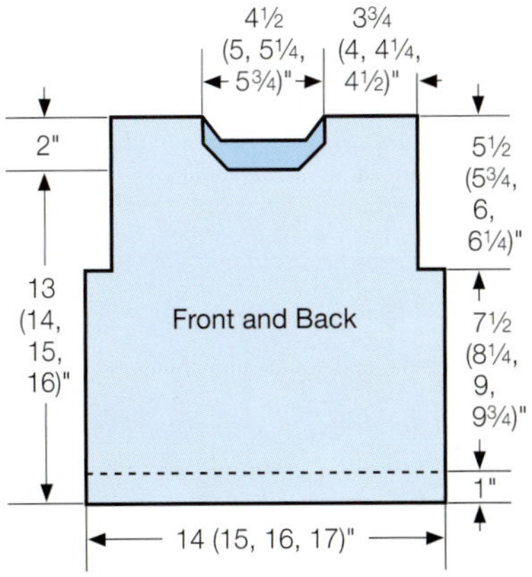

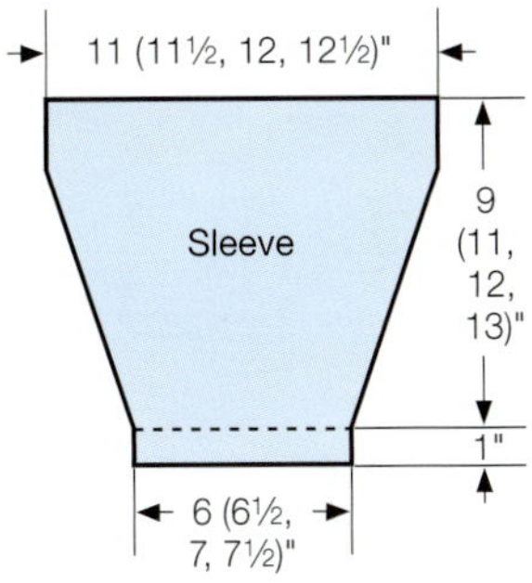

Front measures same length as Back. Place sts on holder for shoulders.

SLEEVE (make 2)

With smaller needles and B, cast on 28 (30, 32, 34) sts. Work in k1, p1 rib for 1", ending on a WS row and inc 4 (4, 6, 6) sts evenly spaced on last row—32 (34, 38, 40) sts. Change to larger needles and St st. Work Inc Row [see Notes] every 4th row 7 (1, 0, 0) times, then every 6th row 2 (8, 3, 0) times, then every 8th row 0 (0, 5, 8) times—50 (52, 54, 56) sts. Work even in St st until piece measures 10 (12, 13, 14)" from beg. Bind off all sts.

FINISHING

With RS tog, join shoulders with 3-needle bind-off.

Neckband: With RS facing, using B and circular needle and starting at right shoulder, pick up and k5 along right Back; k14 (16, 18, 20) sts from Back neck holder; pick up and k5 along left Back; pick up and k14 along left Front; k8 (10, 12, 14) sts from Front neck holder; pick up and k14 along right Front; place marker and join—60 (64, 68, 72) sts. Work k1, p1 rib in rounds for 1". Bind off loosely in rib. Sew Sleeves onto body. Sew side and underarm seams. Weave in loose ends.

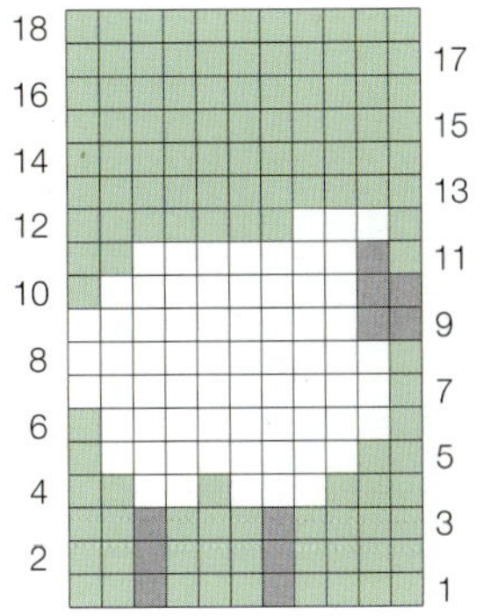

Chart A

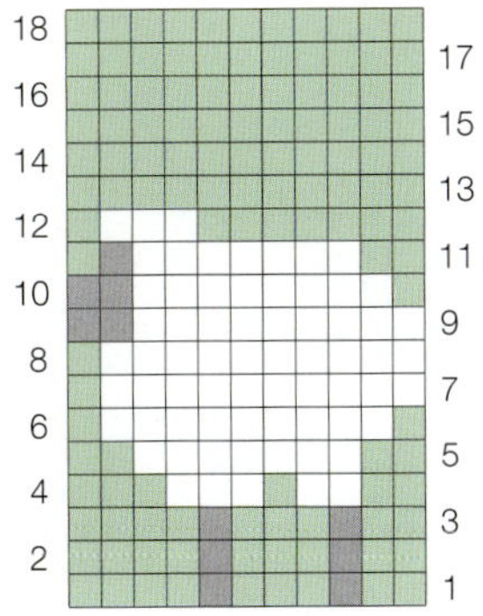

Chart B

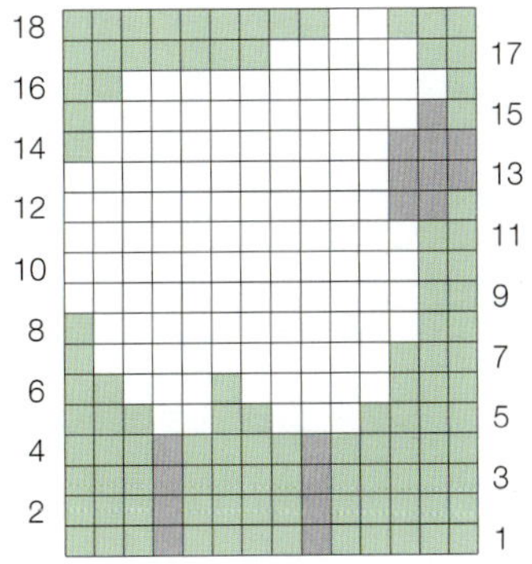

Chart C

cool hats

Everywhere you look, these hip hats are what's happenin' on the guy scene!

DESIGNER: NANCY THOMAS
PHOTOGRAPHER: PERRY STRUSE

SKILL LEVEL
Easy

SIZE
One size fits most adults.

FINISHED MEASUREMENTS
Circumference = 20"
Length = 9" from cast-on edge to top

YARNS
Lion Brand Wool-Ease (Art. 620); 80% acrylic/20% wool; 3 oz. (85 g); 197 yds. (180 m); medium weight
- 1 ball #170 Peacock, #099 Fisherman, or #153 Black (MC)
- 1 ball #153 Black or #102 Ranch Red (A)

NEEDLES & EXTRAS
- Size 8 (5 mm) 16" circular needle
- Size 8 (5 mm) double-pointed needles (dpns)
- Stitch marker
- Blunt-end yarn needle

GAUGE
18 sts and 24 rows = 4" (10 cm) over St st (knit 1 row, purl 1 row).
TAKE TIME TO CHECK YOUR GAUGE.

PATTERN STITCH
STRIPE PATTERN
Rnds 1–4: With A, knit.
Rnds 5–10: With MC, knit.
Rep Rnds 1–10 for pattern.

INSTRUCTIONS
With MC and circular needle, cast on 84 sts. Place marker, join and work 4 rnds in k1, p1 rib. Knit 10 rnds. Work 24 rnds in Stripe Pattern.
Shape crown: With MC only, work decs as follows, changing to dpns when necessary:
Rnd 1: *K2tog, k4; rep from *—70 sts.
Rnds 2, 4, 6, 8: Knit.
Rnd 3: *K2tog, k3; rep from *—56 sts.
Rnd 5: *K2tog, k2; rep from *—42 sts.
Rnd 7: *K2tog, k1; rep from *—28 sts.
Rnd 9: *K2tog; rep from *—14 sts.
Rnd 10: (K2tog) 7 times—7 sts.
Cut yarn. With yarn needle, run tail through rem 7 sts and fasten off. Weave in ends.

buttoned scarf

Practical *and* stylish—what more could you ask of a warm winter scarf? This one fastens with a pom-pom.

DESIGNER: NANCY WYATT PHOTOGRAPHER: JASON WILDE

SKILL LEVEL
Easy

FINISHED MEASUREMENTS
Approx 7×41½"

YARN
Lion Brand Landscapes (Art. 540); 50% wool/50% acrylic; 1¾ oz. (50 g); 55 yds. (50 m); bulky weight

- 3 skeins #277 Country Sunset

NEEDLES & EXTRAS
- Size 13 (9 mm) knitting needles *or size needed to obtain gauge*
- Jumbo pom-pom maker
- Blunt-end yarn needle

GAUGE
2¾ sts and 15 rows over Mistake Rib Pattern = 4" (10 cm).
TAKE TIME TO CHECK YOUR GAUGE.

PATTERN STITCH
MISTAKE RIB PATTERN

Row 1: *K2, p2; rep from *; end k2, p1.
Rep Row 1.

INSTRUCTIONS
Cast on 19 sts. Work in Mistake Rib Pat for 9".

Buttonhole row: Work across 11 sts in pat; bind off the 10th st (9 sts will be on the right needle after bind-off); cont across rem 9 sts in pat.

Next row: Work (k2, p2) twice, k1; join new ball of yarn and work (p2, k2) twice, end p1. Cont to work pat, referring to previous row and using 2 balls for separate sides of opening for 1½".

Next row: Work (k2, p2) twice, k1, cast on 1 st; then work (p2, k2) twice, end p1.
Work rem of scarf in Mistake Rib Pat for 31". Bind off in pat.

FINISHING
Using the same yarn and following the manufacturer's instructions, make a 3½"-diameter pom-pom. With yarn needle and yarn tails from pom-pom, sew pom-pom to the center front of the scarf 9" above the bind-off row on the WS of the scarf.

boy's vest

Here's a sharp V-neck of alternating plain and textured stripes.

DESIGNER: ANN E. SMITH
PHOTOGRAPHERS: SCOTT LITTLE, *OPPOSITE;*
ANDY LYONS, *THIS PAGE*

SKILL LEVEL
Easy

SIZES
Boys' size 6 (8, 10, 12, 14)
The pattern is written for the smallest size with changes for larger sizes in parentheses. When only one number is given, it applies to all sizes.
Note: For ease in working, circle all numbers pertaining to the size you're making.

FINISHED MEASUREMENTS
Chest = 31½ (33½, 35, 37, 39)"
Length =17 (18½, 20, 21½, 23)"

YARNS
Chester Farms Cestari; 100% wool; 4 oz.; 290 yds.; 3-ply lightweight DK weight
- 1 (1, 2, 2, 2) skein(s) Midnight Black (A)
- 1 (1, 2, 2, 2) skein(s) Natural Medium Gray (B)

NEEDLES & EXTRA
- Size 7 (4.5 mm) knitting needles *or size needed to obtain gauge*
- Size 5 (3.75 mm) 16" circular needle
- Blunt-end yarn needle

GAUGE
In Body Pat with larger needles, 17 sts and 22 rows = 4" (10 cm).
TAKE TIME TO CHECK YOUR GAUGE.

SPECIAL ABBREVIATIONS
Sl 1: Sl 1 st pwise with yarn on WS of fabric.
Ssk (slip, slip, knit): Sl next 2 sts kwise, one at a time to right needle, insert tip of left needle into fronts of these 2 sts and k tog.

STITCHES
BORDER: A multiple of 4 sts + 3 (7, 3, 7, 3) sts; a rep of 14 rows
Row 1 (RS): With B, k1 (3, 1, 3, 1); (sl 1, k3) across, ending sl 1, k1 (3, 1, 3, 1).
Row 2: With B, p1 (3, 1, 3, 1); (sl 1, p3) across, ending sl 1, p1 (3, 1, 3, 1).
Row 3: With A, k.
Row 4: With A, p.
Rows 5–8: Rep Rows 1–4.
Rows 9 and 10: With B, rep Rows 1 and 2.
Row 11: With A, k.
Row 12: With A, k.
Row 13: With A, p.
Row 14: With A, p.
Rep Rows 1–14 once more for Border.

BODY PATTERN: A multiple of 8 sts + 3 (7, 3, 7, 3) sts; a rep of 12 rows
Row 1 (RS): With B, k1 (3, 1, 3, 1); (p1, k3) across, ending p1, k1 (3, 1, 3, 1).
Row 2: With B, p1 (3, 1, 3, 1); (k5, p3) across, ending k1, p1 (3, 1, 3, 1).
Rows 3 and 4: With A, rep Rows 1 and 2.
Rows 5 and 6: With B, rep Rows 1 and 2.
Row 7: With A, k1 (3, 1, 3, 1); (p1, k3) across, ending p1, k1 (3, 1, 3, 1).
Row 8: With A, p1 (3, 1, 3, 1), k1; (p3, k5) across, ending p1 (3, 1, 3, 1).
Rows 9 and 10: With B, rep Rows 7 and 8.
Rows 11 and 12: With A, rep Rows 7 and 8. Rep Rows 1–12 for Body Pat.

INSTRUCTIONS
BACK
Beg at lower edge, with larger needles and A, cast on 67 (71, 75, 79, 83) sts. K 1 row, p 1 row, k 1 row. Rep Border Rows 1–14 twice. Begin Body Pat, working to approx 11½ (12½, 13½, 14½, 15½)" from beg, ending with a WS row.
Shape armhole: At each armhole edge, bind off 5 sts once, 3 sts once, 2 sts once, and 1 st 1 (2, 2, 3, 3) time(s)—45 (47, 51, 53, 57) sts. Cont pat to approx 17 (18½, 20, 21½, 23)" from beg, ending with a WS row. With last color used, bind off kwise and loosely.

FRONT
Work as for Back to approx 10½ (11½, 12½, 13½, 14½)" from beg, ending with a WS row.
Shape neck: In pat work first 33 (35, 37, 39, 41) sts; place center st onto a holder; join a new strand and work to end of row. Work sides separately and at the same time as follows:
Row 1: Cont est pat across.
Row 2: Work pat to last 3 sts, k2tog, k1; on next side k1, ssk, pat to end. Rep these 2 rows for 7 (6, 6, 5, 6) times more, then dec as est every 4th row 3 (4, 5, 6, 6) times. AT THE SAME TIME, when piece measures 11½ (12½, 13½, 14½, 15½)" from beg, shape armholes as for Back. With 11 (12, 13, 14, 15) sts rem for each shoulder, work to same length as Back, ending with a WS row. With last color used, bind off kwise and loosely.

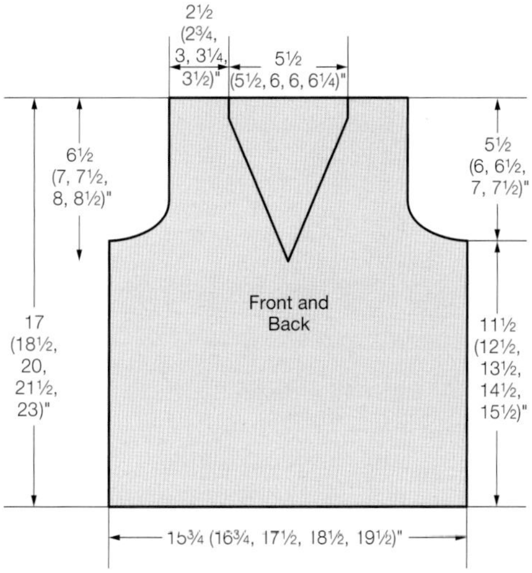

FINISHING
Join shoulder seams.

NECKBAND
With RS facing, using smaller circular needle and B, begin at V-neck and k1 from holder. Pick up and k34 (37, 40, 42, 45) sts evenly spaced to shoulder, 24 (24, 26, 26, 28) sts along back neck, and 34 (37, 40, 42, 45) sts evenly spaced along opposite side of V-neck—93 (99, 107, 111, 119) sts.
Ribbing—Row 1 (WS): P1; (k1, p1) across.
Row 2: K1; (p1, k1) across. Rep Rows 1 and 2 once, then rep Row 1 again. Bind off in ribbing. Cross left side of ribbed band over right side and sew in place.

ARM BAND (make 2)
With the RS facing, using smaller circular needle and color B, pick up and k71 (77, 83, 89, 95) sts evenly spaced around armhole opening. Work Ribbing Rows 1 and 2 as for Neckband; then rep Row 1 again. Bind off in ribbing. Join side seams.

knit basics

BASIC KNITTING TOOLS

Many knitters have discovered the convenience of having a small kit filled with basic knitting accessories—they can quickly move it from one project bag to the next. Here are suggestions for tools to pack in your kit: tape measure, point protectors of assorted sizes, stitch markers, tapestry needle, split ring markers, knitting gauge, stitch holders, cable needles, a row counter, and a crochet hook for picking up the occasional dropped stitch.

SKILL LEVELS

BEGINNER: Projects for first-time knitters are labeled "Beginner." These patterns use basic stitches, minimal shaping, and very simple finishing.

EASY: Projects labeled "Easy" use basic stitches, repetitive stitch patterns, simple color changes, and simple shaping and finishing.

INTERMEDIATE: Projects labeled "Intermediate" use a variety of techniques, such as basic cables and lace or color patterns, with midlevel shaping and finishing.

EXPERIENCED: Projects labeled "Experienced" use advanced techniques and stitches, with detailed shaping and refined finishing.

FOR MORE HELP

Visit www.YarnStandards.com for a downloadable booklet with knitting information compiled by the Craft Yarn Council of America. The booklet contains standard sizing information, abbreviations, yarn weights and sizes, and more.

MAKING A GAUGE SWATCH

Using the recommended needles and yarn, cast on a few more stitches than the number indicated by the gauge printed on the yarn band for 4" (10 cm). Work the pattern for at least 4". Loosely bind off or remove the swatch from the needles. Place a ruler over the swatch; count the number of stitches across 1" and the number of rows down 1", including fractions of stitches or rows. If you have too many stitches and rows, switch to larger needles; if you have too few stitches, use smaller needles.

KNITTING NEEDLE SIZES

(U.S. sizes)

Size 1 = 2.25 mm
Size 2 = 2.75 mm
Size 3 = 3.25 mm
Size 4 = 3.5 mm
Size 5 = 3.75 mm
Size 6 = 4 mm
Size 7 = 4.5 mm
Size 8 = 5 mm
Size 9 = 5.5 mm
Size 10 = 6 mm
Size 10½ = 6.5 mm
Size 11 = 8 mm
Size 13 = 9 mm
Size 15 = 10 mm
Size 17 = 12.75 mm
Size 19 = 15 mm
Size 35 = 19 mm

ABBREVIATIONS

The abbreviations used throughout this book plus other common ones—are listed below.

approx	approximately
beg	begin(ning)(s)
bet	between
ch	chain
cn	cable needle
cont	continue
dec	decrease(s)(ing)
dpn(s)	double-pointed needle(s)
est	established
FP	front post
inc	increase(s)(ing)
k or K	knit
kwise	as if to knit
k2tog	knit two stitches together (right-slanting decrease when right side is facing you)
lp(s)	loop(s)
M1	make one stitch; knit into back loop of running stitch
p or P	purl
pat	pattern
pm	place marker
psso	pass slipped stitch over
p2sso	pass two slipped stitches over
p2tog	purl two stitches together (right-slanting decrease when right side is facing you)
pwise	as if to purl
rem	remain(s)(ing)
rep	repeat(s)(ing)
rev sc	reverse single crochet
rnd(s)	round(s)
RS	right side(s) of work
sc	single crochet
sl	slip
sm	slip marker
ssk	(slip, slip, knit) slip two stitches, one at a time knitwise, insert left needle and knit two together (left-slanting decrease when right side is facing you)
ssp	(slip, slip, purl) slip two stitches, one at a time knitwise, pass back to left needle, purl together through back loops (left-slanting decrease when right side is facing you)
st(s)	stitch(es)
St st	stockinette stitch (knit 1 row, purl 1 row)
tbl	through the back loop(s)
tog	together
WS	wrong side(s) of work
wyib	with yarn in back
wyif	with yarn in front
yo	yarn over
( )	work instructions within parentheses in the place directed and the number of times indicated
[ ]	work step in brackets the number of times indicated
*	repeat the instructions following the single asterisk as directed

KNITTING TECHNIQUES

CABLE CAST-ON

STEP 1 Make a slip knot on the left needle.

STEP 1

STEP 2 Working into the loop of the knot, knit a stitch; transfer it to the left needle.

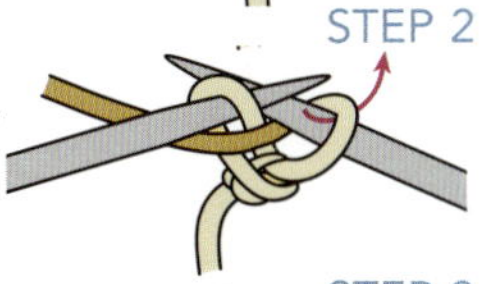
STEP 2

STEP 3 Insert the right needle between those two stitches. Knit a stitch and transfer it to the left needle. Repeat this step for each additional stitch.

STEP 3

LONG-TAIL CAST-ON

Estimate a yarn tail length that is three times the length of what the cast-on edge will be.

STEP 1 Make a slip knot this distance from the yarn end and place it on the right needle.

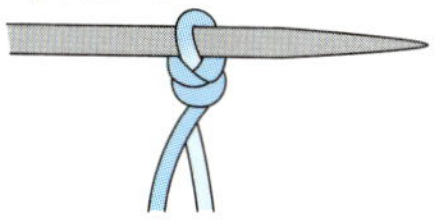
STEP 1

STEP 2 *Position thumb and index finger between the two strands of yarn. Close the other fingers into the palm of your hand and securely hold the yarn.

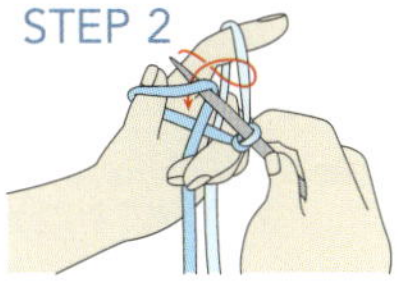
STEP 2

STEP 3 Moving in an upward direction, insert the needle under the yarn on the thumb and into the loop that's formed around the thumb. Take the needle over the top of the yarn in front of the index finger and guide it down into the thumb loop—the strand of yarn from the index finger easily moves along with the needle. Pull the strand through the thumb loop, making a new loop on the right needle.

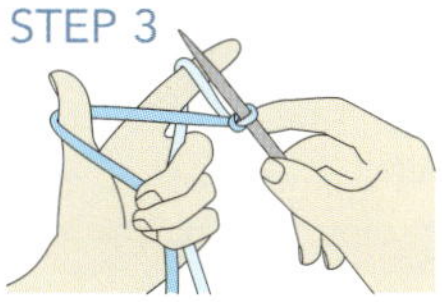
STEP 3

STEP 4 Drop the yarn around the thumb, and spread your index finger and thumb to tighten the loop on the needle—one cast-on stitch is made. Repeat from * to make a second cast-on stitch.

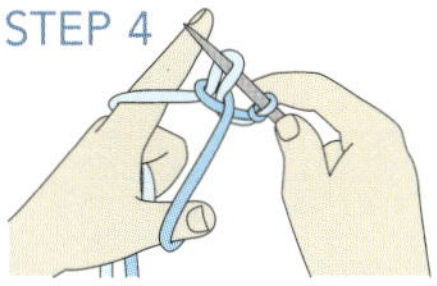
STEP 4

3-NEEDLE BIND-OFF

With RS together, hold in one hand two needles with an equal number of stitches on each and with points in same direction.

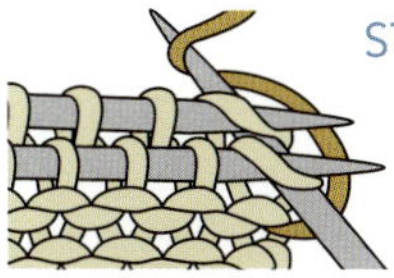
STEP 1

STEP 1 Using a third needle of same size, knit together one stitch from each needle.

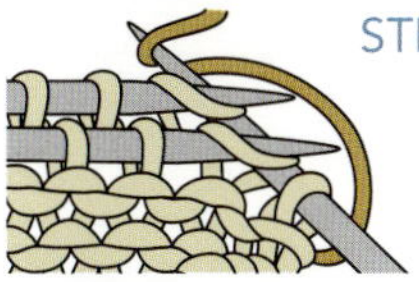
STEP 2

STEPS 2 & 3 *Knit together the next stitch from each needle, pass the first stitch worked over the second stitch to bind off; repeat from * across to bind off all stitches.

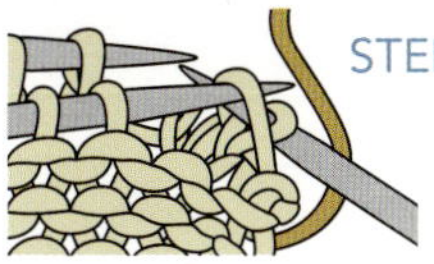
STEP 3

M1 (make one stitch)

Work an increase by lifting the horizontal thread lying between the needles and placing it onto the left needle. Work the new stitch through the back loop.

KNIT STITCH

STEP 1 With yarn in back, insert the right needle from front to back into the first stitch on the left needle. Notice that the right needle is behind the left needle.

STEP 2 Form a loop by wrapping the yarn under and around the right needle.

STEP 3 Pull the loop through the stitch so the loop is in front of the work.

STEP 4 Slip the first or "old" knit stitch over and off the tip of the left needle, leaving it on the right needle.

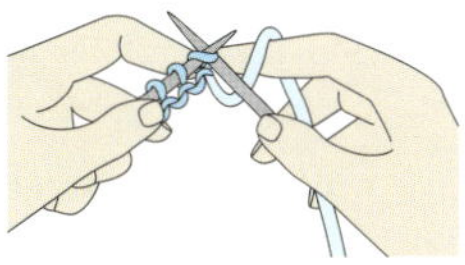
STEP 1

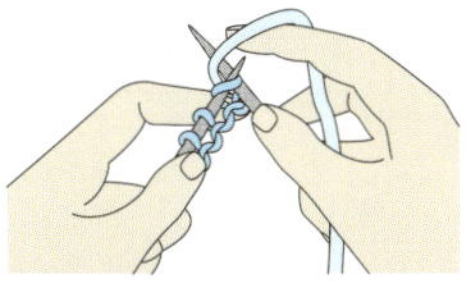
STEP 2

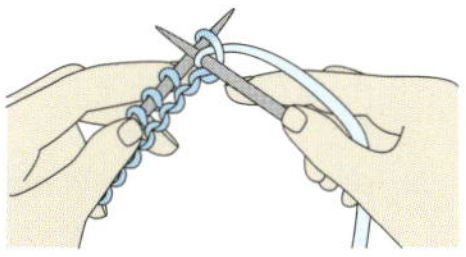
STEP 3

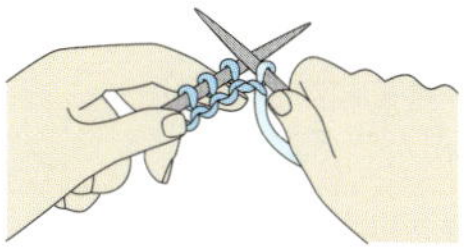
STEP 4

SSK

Slip the next two stitches to the right needle singly and knitwise; insert tip of left needle through the front loop of both stitches and knit them together.

PURL STITCH

STEP 1 With yarn in front of the work, put the right needle from back to front into the first stitch on the left needle.

STEP 2 Form a loop by wrapping the yarn on top of and around the right needle.

STEP 3 Pull the loop through the stitch to make a new purl stitch.

STEP 4 Slip the first or "old" purl stitch over and off the tip of the left needle, leaving it on the right needle.

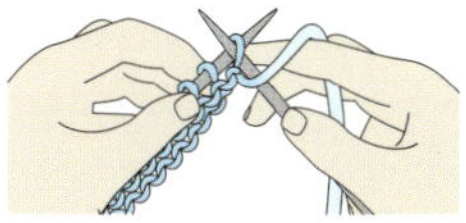
STEP 1

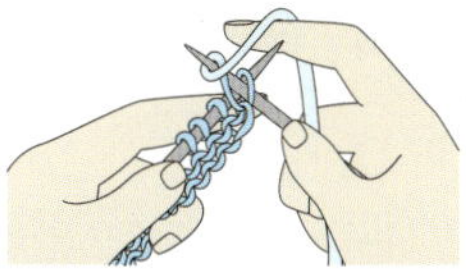
STEP 2

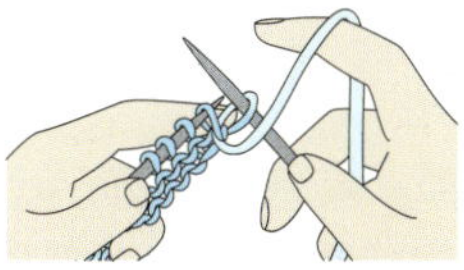
STEP 3

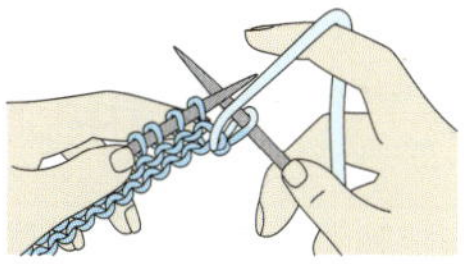
STEP 4

Better Homes and Gardens®
Creative Collection™

Editorial Director
Gayle Goodson Butler

Editor-in-Chief
Beverly Rivers

Executive Editor Karman Wittry Hotchkiss

Art Director
Brenda Drake Lesch

Contributing Editorial Manager
Heidi Palkovic

Contributing Editor Laura Holtorf Collins
Contributing Design Director Tracy DeVenney
Contributing Graphic Designer Kim Hopkins
Copy Chief Mary Heaton
Contributing Copy Editor Pegi Bevins
Proofreader Dana Schmidt
Administrative Assistant Lori Eggers

Senior Vice President
Bob Mate

Publishing Group President
Jack Griffin

Meredith
CORPORATION

Chairman and CEO William T. Kerr
President and COO Stephen M. Lacy

In Memoriam
E. T. Meredith III (1933–2003)